Beyond Illusions

Discovering Your True Nature

Dan Desmarques

22 Lions

Beyond Illusions: Discovering Your True Nature

Written by Dan Desmarques

Copyright © 2024 by Dan Desmarques. All Rights Reserved.

No part of this publication may be reproduced or transmitted in any form or by any means, electronic or mechanical, including photocopy, recording, or any information storage and retrieval system now known or to be invented, without permission in writing from the publisher, except by a reviewer who wishes to quote brief passages in connection with a review written for inclusion in a magazine, newspaper, or broadcast.

Contents

Introduction — VII

1. Chapter 1: Uncovering the Self — 1
2. Chapter 2: The Burden of Ignorance — 5
3. Chapter 3: Embracing Uncertainty — 9
4. Chapter 4: Desire and Fear — 13
5. Chapter 5: The Illusion of Control — 17
6. Chapter 6: The Alchemy of Connection — 21
7. Chapter 7: The Paradox of Love — 25
8. Chapter 8: Dreams and Reality — 29
9. Chapter 9: The Price of Success — 33
10. Chapter 10: The Mirage of Life — 37
11. Chapter 11: The Veils of Reality — 41
12. Chapter 12: The Mirror of Self-Reflection — 45
13. Chapter 13: The Path to Authenticity — 49
14. Chapter 14: Inner Transformation — 53
15. Chapter 15: The Metamorphosis of the Soul — 57

16.	Chapter 16: The Unseen Path to Wholeness	61
17.	Chapter 17: The Power of Positive Change	65
18.	Chapter 18: Reinvention and Truth	69
19.	Chapter 19: The Nature of Hope	73
20.	Chapter 20: The Transformation of Love	77
21.	Chapter 21: Transcending Transition	81
22.	Chapter 22: Love and Change	85
23.	Chapter 23: The Transformative Power of Observation	89
24.	Chapter 24: The Wisdom of Solitude	93
25.	Chapter 25: The Loneliness of Enlightenment	97
26.	Chapter 26: The Lighted Path	101
27.	Glossary of Terms	105
28.	References	109
29.	Book Review Request	111
30.	About the Author	113
31.	Also Written by the Author	115
32.	About the Publisher	125

Introduction

In a world saturated with distractions and superficial pursuits, the search for authentic happiness and self-love can often feel elusive. "Beyond Illusions: Discovering Your True Nature" is a profound exploration of the human experience, delving into the depths of our identities, the nature of our relationships, and the search for meaning in a chaotic world.

Through a series of introspective chapters, readers are invited on a journey of self-discovery, confronting fundamental aspects of their existence. From the complexities of identity and the nature of love to the transformative power of dreams and the pursuit of happiness, this book challenges conventional wisdom and societal norms.

With unflinching honesty and keen insight, the author explores the paradoxes of human nature and the struggles we face in our quest for fulfillment. More than a book, Beyond Illusions is a call to action, encouraging readers to shed the illusions that bind them, embrace their true selves, and find meaning and happiness in a world that often seems indifferent to their struggles.

Whether you are looking for answers to life's big questions or simply a fresh perspective, this book offers a unique and thought-provoking exploration of the human experience. It invites you to question the status quo, challenge the narratives that have shaped your life, and embark on a journey of self-discovery that will ultimately lead you to a deeper understanding of your true nature.

Chapter 1: Uncovering the Self

Our sense of self is intricately woven into our identity-who we are, how we perceive the world, and the meaning we give to our lives. This identity shapes our understanding of existence and our overall sense of purpose. As we journey through life, we encounter a world where the lines between the ordinary and the extraordinary are blurred, and the mundane and the magical coexist. Along the way, our certainties dissolve, inviting us to appreciate existence without expectations.

Those who dare to venture beyond this state of being, to confront the core questions of our existence and redefine our understanding of the world, are invited to explore the most fundamental aspects of the human condition. True knowledge can only come through true understanding. The more we cling to our assumptions in the face of confusion, the more we perpetuate the reasons that justify further reincarnations. We suffer not because of what is ending, but because of our attachments to things that we knew would end and that we arrogantly assumed would not affect our beliefs.

Life has always been a struggle, a constant battle, and fundamental change occurs only when we make the decision to stop passively accepting what others have created and want for us, and instead begin to pursue what we want most. This struggle can be harder than we imagine, not necessarily because of the obstacles we can't overcome, but rather because of the incessant number of people trying to stop us, many of whom we thought were on our side and loved us.

It may take you a long time to realize that people can't love because they don't understand what love is. When people claim to love someone, they are attaching a need and an expectation to that person. They are saying that they want to be specifically validated and accepted by that person. But they don't know what love is; they simply and arrogantly want to believe that they do, because they don't want to confront their ignorance and selfishness in the process of peeling back the layers of their false selves.

I have come to realize that the world has always been a struggle for survival, a truth hidden beneath the veneer of illusion that everyone seems to embrace. But this same world has been made this way because of the lack of empathy and the absolute selfishness of many, as well as their animalistic tendency to value pleasure over meaning. People do not care about living without pleasure and will gladly let go of anything that does not bring them pleasure. Many call this being social and entertaining, but I call it being spiritually empty.

Socially, everyone smiles and presents a facade of happiness, but when they are alone, the reality becomes much harsher and depression ends up being a never ending barrage of demons in their head telling them how miserable they are. Some resort to suicide, others find solace in alcohol, and many more succumb to tears when the distractions of television or movies fail to provide the escape they so desperately crave. This is a world of profound madness, a truth I have discovered in my travels around the globe.

It is foolish to look for love on a planet where people love no one, not even themselves. Instead, respect and empathy should be the priority. I have no love for those who do not respect me and show me no empathy. I would be crazy to love such people. And if they say they love me, they are lying. If they think they love me, they are crazy. If they cannot respect me and my views, they cannot love me. They can only love the idealization they have of me, the illusion of me in their minds. If they fall out of love, it is because they can no longer maintain that illusion.

It is foolish to try to rationalize the harmful actions of others and then forgive them because of their life experiences or challenges. People have a choice at every moment; being evil is a choice, and it needs to be stopped and removed from society, just like a robber who somehow asks to be imprisoned to prevent himself from robbing because he cannot control himself.

Of course, we cannot equate robbing food with threatening the lives of others with a gun, but do people even understand the difference? I have often been asked why I tell people to give money to a robber instead of trying to fight him, as if they do not already do that to their government and bank in the form of fees and taxes. People are too unconscious to see the many ways in which they are robbed of their wealth, and then they complain about petty things, even risking their lives for them, while they would risk nothing if the bank took their house for lack of payment.

Chapter 2: The Burden of Ignorance

The world is challenging because people often resist change and cling to their beliefs, even when those beliefs are harmful. Trying to help others by offering advice on how to avoid suffering, improve their health, or prevent disease often leads to resentment, ridicule, and insults. People may accuse you of various wrongdoings simply to avoid facing the truth you present. If you want to lose friends quickly, start offering effective help to everyone, and soon you will find yourself isolated.

It is commonly said that success requires taking risks, but the greatest and most avoided risk is making others uncomfortable by presenting facts and challenging their beliefs. In my encounters with various religious communities, I have witnessed firsthand the anger and hostility that can arise when people feel their beliefs are threatened. I was called evil and arrogant simply because I had knowledge that others lacked. This experience shed light on why so many in Europe centuries ago were persecuted and even burned at the stake for reading forbidden books.

There is no inherent danger in pursuing your dreams unless you believe you need the approval of others. The need for approval and validation is directly proportional to the danger you may face. This need can have consequences far beyond what you can imagine, for people rarely show an interest in fulfilling their responsibilities, even when their livelihood depends on it.

Many people believe that everyone has the right to a job and a salary, regardless of their competence. They often do not understand the purpose of their work or even why they have the things they have. I have observed that a significant number of people seem to dislike their customers, which begs the question: Why should I patronize a coffee shop where the waiters are rude, as is often the case throughout Europe? And why should café and supermarket waiters in Europe deserve a job if they do not value their work or their customers?

I firmly believe that automation, such as vending machines, could increase the profits of these businesses for obvious reasons: Machines do not treat customers rudely and can do repetitive tasks efficiently. Besides, why should people with such jobs fear death if they do not value life?

When I first entered the workforce, I quickly realized that my work was not valued, and I was often fired for being too competent. It became clear that people resent those who know what they are doing when they do not. It is not easy to keep a job in a world filled with delusional and irresponsible people. I often felt like I was in a mental hospital, tiptoeing around patients with mental disorders, where daily rituals and perceptions are more important than the actual work that justifies their salary.

I realized that this paradigm exists worldwide, except in societies that prioritize results over social validation, leading to superior productivity and wealth. Had I known then what I know now, I would have followed the guidelines and principles I now share with others. The problem is that I have not found anyone who shares the same views, and those who do listen to me often insult and ignore me because they are too entrenched in their beliefs to see the value of what I am sharing.

If I could go back in time, I would tell my former self that people are often misguided and what they say has little value. It is truly better to put hope in the unknown than to trust the minds of the arrogant, especially when they use their own debased and uninformed religious interpretations to condition others to follow them.

If we need to forgive someone, let us start with ourselves, for we know nothing and do not recognize our own mistakes when we assume that we do in comparison to others. In fact, hope has done more for me than any human being I have ever met, giving me the wings to pursue a better life faster and beyond the mundane limitations of others. It has also helped me reach deep within myself to find who I am.

Chapter 3: Embracing Uncertainty

I have observed that societies do not change as much as one might expect. Decades and even centuries go by, yet many things remain the same, a testament to people's stubborn resistance to change. New generations often reflect the laziness and ignorance of their predecessors, proudly following in their footsteps, conditioned by the same false beliefs passed down from parents and grandparents. This continues despite the fact that we live in a world that is fundamentally different from what we are told about it.

However, what I have fought so hard for in the face of such adversity has become the foundation of my faith in pursuing my dreams. To suggest that my current outcome is solely determined by my struggles is a simplistic way to rationalize life, as many endure similar hardships and succumb to far less. The truth is that I have always been a peaceful and cheerful individual, worn down by the relentless cruelty and indifference of the world around me. Had circumstances been different, I would have been myself much sooner.

This realization has led me to understand that true success is not measured by the risks we take, but by the resilience and strength we show in the face of adversity. It is a delicate balance, but ultimately it is not the risks we take that define us, but the choices we make in the aftermath. Those choices are determined by how much and how fast we can learn, for we only see when we know. If there is nothing to help us in this quest, we must read voraciously and abundantly.

This is exactly what I have done - first to know myself, then to know the world, and finally to create my own reality, one that others now claim is not real. It is ironic that once you separate yourself from the reality of others by creating your own, you are called a liar. Your truth becomes a lie to those who have succumbed to their own lies and, by agreeing with those same lies, claim that they are truths for that reason alone.

I realize now that there is no end to the struggle because there is no end to the immense madness and ignorance of the world. We can only try to be prepared for it and live apart from it. The alternative is illusion - pretending to like people who don't like us, struggling to understand those who have no interest in understanding us or improving themselves, and living in a constant state of fear for no other reason than to have an existence that feels insulting to those who don't like theirs.

Many believe that if they cannot find a way to be accepted and loved by others, they cannot find love for themselves, but the opposite is always true. Without this love, which we must learn to cultivate within ourselves and for ourselves, we risk sleeping through despair, only to wake up each morning with a new sense of purpose that often fizzles out.

Great meaning, I have found, comes only when we do something that transcends ourselves. Having children is one way, but another equally important way, which only altruists can understand, is to work for the unborn, to share wisdom with them, even if we may never meet.

The greatest artist always lets his art outlive him. But many people on this planet are so driven by the desire for conflict that they are far from ever realizing the value of building a life, seeking knowledge, or finding beauty. The romanticized idea of war, of nationalistic ideals, of conflict as a noble endeavor, is inherently narcissistic and a sign of a very sick society. It assumes that one's cause is so righteous, so pure, that it justifies the taking of lives and the destruction of worlds.

The only war worth fighting is a war of preservation. It is a battle to defend our integrity and the integrity of those who share our spiritual beliefs. It is a recognition that certain values are worth fighting for. Today's wars are being fought in the realm of mind and spirit. But those who don't recognize them don't know that they are already dead. We are in a time when the most powerful conflicts are those of ideologies, of beliefs, of narratives, where we have to find the truth among many lies.

This is a war for the soul of the human race, a struggle to define our collective identity and common destiny. The weapons we need today are those of clarity, discernment, and purpose, honed and sharpened by years of observation, reflection, and introspection.

They cut through falsehood and delusion, through lies and folly. They are not weapons of destruction, but tools of illumination, shedding light on the darkness that has taken root in our society.

Chapter 4: Desire and Fear

Honesty and authenticity have the power to change the course of history, inspire revolutions, topple empires, and create new worlds. They shape our perception of reality, our understanding of the past, and our vision of the future. This struggle transcends opinions, beliefs, and egos. Although the future may be uncertain, with love for ourselves, our existence, and our ideas of a better life, and with courage and conviction, we can change the course of history and create a brighter tomorrow.

This future may elude the masses who, in their frightening apathy, may not even see it, instead shutting themselves off to a reality more suited to their low state of consciousness. Indeed, not everyone operates on the same spectrum of life. Many people see life only through the lens of their own experience and reinterpret everything they see accordingly.

This means that although we all have access to the same information, we all experience it differently within ourselves. But the most fascinating aspect of this is how much people condition themselves through such experiences, for change is often just a choice away-a decision to read, learn, and seek new knowledge.

Few reach the level of consciousness that awakens them to this necessary journey; instead, they succumb to their own beliefs and become strongly attached to them. Nothing makes this more obvious than the realities of poverty, where everyone has a cell phone and wastes time watching nonsense instead of educating themselves. It is an interesting paradox that the rich tend to read the most, while the poor need education much more than the rich.

In the vibrant landscape of my youth, I was a dreamer, a reckless adventurer in the realm of desire. But my dreams were often ridiculed by those limited by their own lack of understanding. Although I was doing the right thing, I was often told I was wrong by those who were on the wrong path in life themselves. It was not until I read widely that I realized that the reality I was creating for myself did not match the reality I was experiencing. I understood then that my life's journey could not include the reality I knew if I truly wanted to make such dreams come true.

In the end, I made many things possible, except those I chose to abandon - a decision that was not a surrender, but a strategic redirection and realignment of energies based on the opportunities I encountered. It is truly foolish to think you can do anything you want on this planet without considering its limitations, but many see this as cynicism, simply because it requires a dose of reality they are unwilling to face.

We are rarely judged by our character, but always by the things we have acquired, because society values those who win, not those who struggle or their personality traits. But the destination, the goal, is only the culmination of an internal and difficult process of transformation, a footnote in the great narrative of our lives. Indeed, to define one's existence in terms of others is to invite despair.

I have come to understand the things others consider valuable as mere accessories, choosing instead to rely on the things within my control-what I know, what I want, and how capable I am of achieving my desires. And though the future is largely uncertain, I face it with hope in my heart, for only then does life have meaning.

Love, for all its romantic appeal, is an ephemeral concept, difficult to quantify and often misunderstood. Sex, on the other hand, is a primal force, a driving instinct that underpins our existence. It is the foundation upon which our psyche is built, the engine that drives our behavior.

Sigmund Freud, controversial as he may be, understood this. He recognized that our sexual instincts dominate our unconscious, shaping our desires and motivations. We begin life seeking nourishment, the comfort of the breast, and as we grow, this instinct transforms into a drive for connection, for pleasure, for procreation. The satisfaction of this drive is a fundamental measure of our well-being, reflected even in the way we move, the way we carry ourselves.

Some idealists proclaim the primacy of love, claiming that it is more important than war. But they are misunderstood because they dare not speak the truth: that the higher ideal, the force that truly shapes our existence, is sex. It is the urge to merge, to connect, to create. It is the impulse that drives us to seek others, to form bonds, to build communities.

This is not to diminish the power of love, but to recognize it as a manifestation of something more primal. In fact, love has little to do with most people's attraction. It is sex that drives us, that shapes us, that makes us who we are. The only thing that can surpass this primal force is an energy that aligns us with the divine in the form of uplifting works of art.

Chapter 5: The Illusion of Control

The most accomplished artists find in their art a form of self-satisfaction that, if not properly nurtured, can turn into addiction, depression, and anxiety. Beneath the surface lies a deeper desire: the desire to connect, to communicate thoughts and feelings, and to embrace our collectivity as one. When a viewer or reader engages with an artist's work, a bond is forged, and this connection, this communion of minds, is the ultimate realization of the artist's instinct.

Love, it is often said, is the greatest force in the world, but love does not exist in a vacuum. Before love is sex, the primal drive that gives love its context and meaning, and after love is the desire for expression. The world, with its intellectual pursuits and lofty ideals, often overlooks this fundamental truth. To deny the importance of pleasure or human connection is to deny the very essence of our being.

When we move away from the divine, we move away from our own nature, and the consequences come in the form of despair, often monetized by those who seek to profit from our isolation and frustration with life. In a world with so many lonely people, there has never been a greater opportunity for businesses to fill the needs once met by marriage and family relationships. Anxiety, depression, insecurity and loneliness are now highly profitable emotions.

To see this reality is not to be a cynic, but to embrace the challenges of the vast majority, most of whom are on their way to other, deeper challenges, financial in nature. Wealth is inextricably linked to how we feel about ourselves. If you don't believe that, try to feel motivated and productive when you feel lonely, apathetic and miserable.

The obsession that people seem to have with happiness and quick results comes with dissatisfaction and a lack of willingness to work. People don't want to be told that they have to work harder for their dreams, and so a great dichotomy looms on the horizon between those who have it all and those who are homeless or close to it.

In a world rapidly connected by ideas and emotions, those who can best express themselves in clear and original ways will lead the rest into the future. We see this clearly through podcasters and social media influencers, terms that until recently were essentially unknown and not so popularized. Art in its various forms is following this trend, with painters, musicians, and writers making more money than ever before.

If these things frighten many, it is only because they challenge their worldview, their religious dogmas, and their need to keep their reality the same. Fear of change always masks the need for stagnation, and stagnation, like dogma, is a characteristic of dark energies that often violently resist any positive innovation. We only have to look at the vast number of innovative scientists with alternative but natural energy sources and homeopaths with natural cures for highly profitable diseases who are constantly silenced or discredited by those in fundamentally corrupt industries to know that this is true.

The greatest mistake of declining civilizations is to confuse the divine and love itself with mere physical acts and personal results, for without love such acts and results are empty and meaningless. True love requires a harmony of mind, heart and soul - deep empathy, mutual understanding and acceptance.

Historically, the idea that intimacy is an extension of commitment made sense because it was inextricably linked to potential consequences and responsibilities. In time, people will understand that the objects of their desires are not as important as the feelings they long for. Only then will they truly grasp love and happiness, not as fleeting emotions or commodities, but as an enduring state of being that strengthens the soul. They will appreciate beauty, not as a passing fad, but as a manifestation of that which uplifts and inspires.

Without love and happiness, the world can indeed seem a dreary place. But too often, people try to fill the void within by devoting their time to respectable careers, hoping to gain validation from society. However, this realization often comes too late, after status has been lost and they lack the energy, knowledge, or adaptability to change their path. They find themselves equipped for a world that no longer exists.

In this way, early rejection, frustration, and failure can be a blessing, nudging us more quickly toward the life we truly desire, as if the universe were guiding us toward our destiny. These experiences can serve as catalysts for growth, pushing us to face our fears and embrace the uncertainty that comes with pursuing our dreams. By accepting that control is often an illusion, we can find the courage to let go and trust in the journey, knowing that each step brings us closer to our true selves.

Chapter 6: The Alchemy of Connection

Prayer and dreams are acknowledgements that we do not have all the answers. It is arrogant to assume that we know the path to our dreams when we ask for help. Prayer requires surrender and faith that the unknown steps ahead will lead us to where we want to go. We cannot control the journey; we can only determine the destination.

For many years, I believed that my ability to achieve goals made me unstoppable. I failed to align my aspirations with my true self and sought external validation and approval. After numerous unfulfilling jobs, I realized that I needed to create a meaningful career. I firmly believe that the meaning of life lies in the pursuit of our creative and spiritual desires. To live only for the respect of others is to live an empty life.

The contemplation of death brings this into sharp focus - no one is so important that they will not be forgotten. Therefore, it is wise to create a life of meaning rather than squander it in search of social validation. Actions that go against our spirit to prioritize validation and pleasure can be considered self-deception. Any teaching that denies our awareness of this truth is flawed.

True spiritual knowledge guides us to become better individuals, not slaves to dogma. Many struggle with inadequacy and detachment because they lack this understanding. They dream of other lives, not realizing that the answers lie within, accessible through self-reflection and spiritual exploration. Through faith and self-knowledge we can create a life of meaning and purpose.

I love the life I have, and I'd rather love my life than have people's respect for a life that doesn't satisfy me. This should be the motto for everyone, but few have the ability to grasp the meaning of choice or freedom. The typical question I get when I visit a new country is, "Why are you here?" As if our decision always depends on some random and external outcome outside of ourselves, as if we have no capacity to be autonomous and choose the course of our destiny. People ask this question because they can't imagine any other possibility.

When I answer that I chose to be in a country for no particular reason, they are confused, as if that were not possible. Some angrily repeat that I must have a reason because no one travels without a reason. They are so immersed in their own madness that they would rather fight to protect it than learn anything new about their limitations.

As a child, when life did not make much sense to me, I looked for reasons, and I certainly did not find them in others. But when the desire for death comes swiftly and unexpectedly, it brings with it a storm of change, a whirlwind that sweeps away the familiar and leaves behind a landscape altered in unpredictable ways. No wonder, then, that many who have embraced their frustrations have become artists, wielding their brushes and pens like weapons against the encroaching darkness. It is as if that which allows us to escape the world also gives us a deeper purpose for continuing to live in it.

In my own journey, I have immersed myself in readings from many spiritual sources, both ritualistic and empirical, dogmatic and occult in their foundations, and from these disparate sources I have accumulated a wealth of knowledge that has guided me through the labyrinth of life and the lies that many still believe. And yet, despite the depth and breadth of my learning, I find myself on a plateau, a barren wasteland where the winds of despair howl ceaselessly. This is because the masses insist on their collective lies, arrogantly refusing to learn and change or respect those who have chosen a different path. The masses have no sympathy for freedom and the rebellion of independent thought, and they show it with their contempt, disrespect, and rejection of those who seek such a path. This is why the truth inevitably isolates us.

This agony that gnaws at the core of our being limits our ability to appreciate all that we have, even though I know full well that I would not have it if I sought the paths that others have envisioned. It is a strange thing, this emptiness that fills the void left by our dreams once they are realized, but in this world it is the price to be paid for a higher realization and understanding of the mysteries of life. Perhaps this is why those who knew more than the average appreciated the company of a cat or a dog more than that of a human.

Chapter 7: The Paradox of Love

The world, in all its glory and despair, is a canvas upon which we paint our own reality. We navigate this canvas with awareness, focusing on what is truly important while being mindful of what is merely degrading. It is through humble submission to our faith that we unlock the power to shape our reality, regardless of the skepticism of others.

I have accomplished countless feats that others thought impossible, so I am often puzzled by their attempts to hinder me, but perhaps it is human nature to resist what we do not understand. Those who claim enlightenment often reveal their dark side when challenged. My experience with religious organizations has shown me the ugliness that can lurk beneath the surface, and I have learned that I cannot reach them without facing their hostility. No matter what evidence is presented, a fool will dismiss it as fantasy, believing his own limited perspective to be the ultimate truth.

It has been a revelation to realize that these fools are everywhere, each pretending to know more than they do. They laugh at what

I know, revealing their ignorance. It is like watching a drunk revel in his own misery, oblivious to the time and consciousness he has lost. But can we feel disrespected by those who know less and insult us because we know more?

Few understand that the power to shape our reality lies not in the hands of some distant deity, but in our own hearts, minds, and souls. Every time they deny this truth, they perpetuate their ignorance. I have come to understand that it is in the act of dreaming - a process often dismissed by the masses as useless - that we develop the neurological pathways necessary for our transformation. This idealization of the self is our true self, for there is no higher self than the one we are striving to become.

Waking up to a view of the ocean in countries I once dreamed of visiting felt surreal, but I cannot explain it to those who do not believe in the power of dreams to come true, especially those who assume they can replicate my life by following a simple formula. Everyone I meet asks how I sell my books, as if that is the key to living the same life. They ignore my background, the knowledge I've accumulated, the wisdom I share in my books, and the diverse fields I've worked in, from business management to teaching at prestigious universities. Their arrogance is as absolute as their ignorance and disrespect. They reduce me to a simplistic assumption, as if I had stumbled upon a magical solution while walking down the street.

The only truly healthy people I have met are those who work harder than anyone else, those who have built and rebuilt their own businesses, and especially those who have gone bankrupt and started over in another field. In other words, only polymaths can understand another polymath. These people are more interested in getting to know me as a person. This is the biggest difference between the masses and the rare exceptions among them. The fools ask me foolish questions while searching for the wrong answers, and the wise offer me coffee and their friendship while humbly expanding their awareness of reality.

The majority does not equal common sense, and the sum of many zeros is still zero. It is wiser to seek guidance in our hearts and in the pages of those who have shared their wisdom than to ask fools to participate in shaping our lives and directing them toward the same results they have received. But people are also so self-absorbed that they are irritated when I ignore their opinions, unable to accept their own uselessness and the nonsense of their words. They are unaware of their unconsciousness. This is why people claim to love others, but do so with conditions and expectations.

True love is unconditional and selfless. It is not about what we can get from others, but what we can give. It is about seeing the best in people even when they cannot see it in themselves. Love is the force that drives us to connect with others, but it is also the emotion that makes us vulnerable, open to heartbreak and pain. To truly embrace love, we must be willing to give, even when we know we may not receive. For it is in this act of giving, in this act of loving, that we find our true self and our true purpose. And so we must embrace the paradox and the life that lies before us. But let us love ourselves first and foremost, for to love the fools is to invite failure.

Chapter 8: Dreams and Reality

The vast majority of people lack self-awareness and cannot see their own ignorance, which is essentially what ignorance is. True intelligence begins when one can recognize and correct one's own mistakes. Until then, one remains unaware of one's unconsciousness, too unaware to realize the extent of one's limitations. But how can you find real answers if you believe that the answers you seek must conform to your preconceived notions?

There is greater wisdom in exploring our ignorance, much like a child learning to use a new toy - in this case, our own mind. It is this metaphysical ability to exteriorize, which children naturally use when they take on the personality of their toys, that allows us to look at ourselves objectively and identify the areas that need change and improvement.

Change always precedes success; it is only the ignorant who refuse to change. This principle has transformed my existence into a stark contrast to the life I once knew. I have gone from working 14 hours a day, Monday through Sunday, at multiple jobs, to not working at all, except when I want to write a new book. Yet I now make far more money than I ever did with all those simultaneous jobs, and far more than I ever dreamed possible.

The realization of my dreams came from an overwhelming and constant investment in working beyond my results, not for my results. The difference was in the direction and values I followed. That is why I can easily ignore what everyone says because I know I am right and they are wrong. But they think I am arrogant for thinking this way, as if agreeing with their ignorance makes me a better person.

This is how the fools try to manipulate your thoughts and change you, using guilt, judgment and punishment as their response. They truly embody arrogance at its finest. But you can't get more arrogant than someone who thinks they are the embodiment of divine values and is willing to destroy your life for their beliefs. We can be thankful that they no longer imprison us, torture us, and burn us alive for disagreeing with them, because they certainly radiate that dark energy and intent.

The tiny apartment where I once laid my head to rest is a distant memory, and the exhaustion that once defined my days, the meals left burning as I succumbed to fatigue, are now echoes of a past that seems almost unreal. For someone who has never taken a vacation or ventured beyond the borders of his own country, this transformation is monumental. And yet, with great success comes great emotional cost, especially when you realize that people hate you more for your accomplishments than when they despised you for having none and struggling to survive.

This kind of envy and resentment really shocked me, precisely because I was never helped in any way other than ignored, even when I faced unemployment and homelessness. Never in years could I have imagined that my friends and family would be so determined to see me fail. But this scenario also explains my struggles, because once I started making my own choices, my life lined up perfectly with what was supposed to be my destiny.

It is incredible how much others will try to stop you based on nothing more than their negative assumptions, but you have to go a long way to see it, and few dare to go beyond the limits of their comfort zone. I have felt the bitter taste of frustration that accompanies the realization of dreams, for it is amazing to enjoy a beautiful place for yourself while others hate you for it.

The realization of my dreams, the achievement of all I had wished for, was not the culmination I had expected, but the beginning of a new, unexpected path. I suddenly understood why so many who reach the pinnacle of success end up in silence and a kind of joy that can't be put into words or properly shared. People often only come back into our lives when they want something from us, I realized. It is a sad result to observe, especially when it comes from people you once respected.

We are led to believe that our lives matter, that our dreams are worth pursuing, only to be confronted with the harsh reality of our own insignificance and the obsession of others to stop us. Our lives do matter, yes, but only to the extent that we give them our own meaning and learn to love ourselves, seeking a form of independence that infuriates and challenges the assumptions of others.

The journey from dream to reality requires that we confront our own ignorance, embrace change, and stand firm in the face of criticism and envy. It is a journey that ultimately leads us to a deeper understanding of ourselves and the world around us. And it is a journey that, despite its challenges, is worth taking because it is the only path to true fulfillment and happiness.

Chapter 9: The Price of Success

Many people I meet around the world still ask me when I plan to get a "real job," as if they expect me to fail and somehow imply that their lives are better than mine. They really mean it because they can't live with the knowledge that I want them to have by thinking differently than they do. Accepting that we fail because of the way we think is a painful reality that many can't face and accept. And yet, they are nothing more than a product of their choices and could live a different life if they chose to.

The last time I spoke to my sister, she insinuated that I was a cruel person for leaving the country to work in another continent. When I confronted her with the fact that she had been offered everything, from studying in a private university to having a place to sleep, while I was expelled and had to sleep on the streets, and that despite all this, I was solving my problems on my own and she was welcome to join me in my new apartment and country, she left angrily in tears.

It is amazing how people react angrily to the truth and yet want you to feel guilty for their selfishness. My two biggest mistakes in life have been expecting people to change and expecting more from them than they show me. I had to lose 20 years of my life to see how wrong my assumption was. Yet death, the great equalizer, awaits us all, a mocking reminder of the futility of our efforts to please others and to waste our existence in a delusional comfort just to avoid confrontation and argument.

Every time I tried to question my intentions toward myself, the illness reminded me that my existence could end at any moment. So why not die as a personality and as a member of society before losing this body? Today, I have achieved enough not to fear death, but this acceptance of the inevitability of my end has also made me more appreciative of life and, as a result, more passionate, ambitious, and hardworking. But because most people are driven by opposite forces, they do not understand why I am this way. I love to work because I love what I do, whether it is reading, researching, or simply sharing knowledge with the world that will outlive me and help many people. I have an altruistic and empathic drive to not want others to suffer as I did, but to find my information to help themselves.

I am much more ambitious than before because I have learned to appreciate freedom, and I know that the more money I have, the faster I can do whatever I want, and the fewer restrictions society places on me. In many countries you can't get a visa, a nice hotel room with a big swimming pool and a plane ticket that will take you across continents with the mindset of a peasant and the scarcity mentality of a 9 to 5 slave with only two weeks vacation a year.

I am more passionate about what I do because I love my life and what I am experiencing with it. Instead of succumbing to norms, cultural narratives and delusional beliefs, I pack up and move on when I don't like the people I meet and they disgust me with their attitudes. This is a luxury many don't have, so they replace their handicap with the need for tolerance, patience, and positive thinking. These ideas, and many others like them, were created to satisfy the weak and the poor because they can't fight back against the system they are in.

It is the same when Christians tell you that it is better to be poor than rich, because they themselves have no idea how to acquire wealth, except to plunder the resources of other nations and their gold, as the Vatican and the Europeans have been doing all over the world for two thousand years in the name of Christian values. It is a stupid people on a large scale, promoting stupid ideas. But because they find comfort in the herd, like an ordinary sheep or cow, they think that anyone who doesn't conform must be a wolf - a danger to society.

There is nothing more demonic than the imposition of dogmas that are fundamentally false and lead to misery, which is why Christianity is a perverse and very evil religion. Christianity captivates its members with the same mask the narcissist uses to manipulate victims, and it's no wonder it's full of them. In fact, much of my learning consisted of erasing the Christian parasite from within me. Only then was I free to understand the truth, and only then did I truly understand God. Still, I couldn't help but be in awe whenever I saw a Christian with a narcissistic intention praying to God, because I really wonder how they feel in their heart, not knowing that they are praying to their inner demon. There is really no difference between the narcissistic atheist and the narcissistic Christian except that one thinks his mind is creating random thoughts for him to chew on like a cow chewing grass and the other thinks he is talking to angels.

Chapter 10: The Mirage of Life

The price of success is high, and it often comes with a deep sense of isolation and misunderstanding from those who are unwilling or unable to see the world as it really is. It requires a relentless pursuit of truth, a willingness to confront one's own ignorance, and the courage to stand up to the prevailing narratives and dogmas that seek to control and manipulate. Success in its truest form is not about wealth or status, but about the freedom to live life on one's own terms, to pursue one's passions, and to make a meaningful impact on the world. It is a journey that requires sacrifice and an unyielding commitment to one's values and beliefs. And it is a journey that, despite its challenges, is worth every step.

We owe nothing to anyone in this existence but ourselves, and if we fail to love ourselves and find a life that makes us respect our own existence, we have failed ourselves. No one will judge us for this but ourselves, and we will be reminded of this every morning when we wake up. In fact, it was not until I read the Hindu scriptures that I understood the meaning of surrendering to a higher power, for it is not about seeking rules and rituals, but about finding our true self within ourselves.

Until then, I was still limiting myself to my accomplishments and not seeking beyond that realm of possibility. I wasn't working for God either, but for the approval of people who didn't really care about my accomplishments, only what I represented to them. It took me a while to understand this, and only then was I able to change the content of my thoughts and become more fluid in life, planning less, assuming less about the problems I faced, and allowing myself to explore the unknown, that great void that many avoid.

It is a paradox that the more you seek that which you avoid, the faster you understand yourself and erase the source of your mental barriers. The most difficult of our experiences often hide profound lessons beneath their challenging surfaces. One such lesson is the liberating realization that we are not eternally bound to places or people that do not resonate with our souls; we have the power to chart our own course through this world.

Those who criticize my candid observations often lack the freedom afforded by extensive travel or the courage to speak openly about their own experiences. It is important to understand that the concept of "culture" can sometimes serve as a mask, hiding a collective agreement on flawed values - a democracy of mediocre minds that fosters a national pride resistant to criticism and change.

As I traversed the globe, I encountered cultures that, while rich in history and tradition, left me with a sense of disillusionment. I found individuals who consistently embodied traits of rudeness, deceit, and disrespect. There were always exceptions, but they did not change the overall landscape of my experiences. Racism, for example, is a byproduct of ignorance and lack of self-awareness. It is as absurd as it is tragic when people who themselves bear the physical characteristics of the groups they despise - such as Greeks, Spaniards, and Croats who resemble North African Arabs - claim to hate Muslims because they assume that all Muslims are not white and that they themselves are not brown. This illusion of superiority is not only unfounded but deeply harmful, creating division where there should be unity.

Another of life's most painful illusions is the belief that our friends and family will unconditionally support our changes and adventures. The truth often reveals an undercurrent of jealousy and competition. This realization is a bitter pill to swallow, but it is essential for personal growth. Wisdom and deception are constant companions on our spiritual journey, and we must learn to live with both, recognizing that the path to Ascension is fraught with betrayal, lies and manipulation.

People may beg for help when they are in need, only to despise you when you ask for something in return. They may ask for money but refuse to offer a bowl of rice or a place to rest. True poverty, however, is not the lack of material possessions; it is the lack of kindness, respect, truth, and basic human decency. Some of the most miserable people I have met have also been some of the most offensive, filling their hearts with hatred for those who have more, creating a toxic cycle of negativity. Helping such people can bring bad karma into our lives because it violates divine laws.

Our help is best reserved for those who truly need it - the disabled, the sick, the elderly, innocent children, and those who are helpers themselves. By helping those who truly deserve our help, we cultivate a world that is not only more compassionate, but also more spiritually aligned.

Chapter 11: The Veils of Reality

It is important to maintain a balance between openness and caution, understanding and discernment. We must not allow unpleasant surprises to harden us, nor pleasant ones to lull us into naivety. Instead, we should strive to learn from each experience, to grow with each challenge, and to continually refine our path toward Ascension. Every step we take, every choice we make, is a brushstroke on the canvas of our existence. We are the artists, and it is within our power to create a life of beauty, meaning and truth.

The mirage of life, with its ever-changing landscapes and illusory figures, can be confusing. Yet it is also an invitation to look deeper, to seek understanding, and to forge a path that is authentic and true. The power to create a life of deep joy and purpose lies not in the hands of fate or fortune, but in our own hearts and minds. By embracing this truth, we can transcend the illusions that bind us and find the freedom to live a life that truly resonates with our soul.

Along the way, some people will despise you because you have what they don't and ignore the effort you've put into it. Others will hate you because you don't need them to accomplish things they can't. Some will hate you for not helping them when they have done nothing to warrant it. And others will continue to pretend to be someone they are not, wasting years of your life before you see the truth in their hearts. But perhaps because I understand this so well, I often see through others better than their own family members.

For example, I once met a Filipina whose mother I described as despicable, a woman who didn't really love her daughter. At first the daughter disagreed, but months later she confessed that her mother had called her a useless whore for dating a foreigner and not sending money to the family. This mother saw her daughter as a commodity, a means to finance the family's misery. Ironically, being a "useless whore" in this context meant submitting to her mother's wishes, which she did out of guilt.

The true poverty of Filipinos is not financial but spiritual; they live in a land of opportunity and yet choose to eat garbage and dog food. If you want to see misery, go to the Philippines. It's one of the most miserable cultures in the world, plagued by corruption and the worst food in Asia. Their government officials are corrupt and demand money to do their jobs, as if paying to leave the country isn't scam enough. What reason does anyone have to visit this decadent culture of misery, corruption and despair?

Filipinos often ask me if I believe in zombies, as if they weren't the next best thing. Another level below their current poverty is cannibalism. And while I haven't seen the entire globe to make definitive conclusions about any nation, I've never met a single person who needs money and wants to work. Many think they should get money for no other reason than their communist and mentally deficient mindset.

Another Filipino admitted that his family demanded that he share his wealth with them for no other reason than he had more. He was angry because he worked extremely hard for what he had, even reading all my books when he didn't have much to eat and his family told him not to. But you can't respect people who try to stop you and then want a piece of your results. He resolved the situation by moving to another city, away from them, and avoiding uncomfortable conversations by turning off online communication. Still, people find it offensive when you tell them that your results come from hard work, because it's not the answer they want. But why should they deserve more than the same contempt they show others?

If I have never met a person who has asked for help but wants to work, I must say that certain conscious karmic choices lead to misery. More than karma, it is a direct cause of selfishness that leads people to their misery. For example, I once gave money to a poor American in Macedonia, and after I gave him enough for one meal, he arrogantly said it wasn't much and ridiculed me. I regretted helping him because such a decadent soul deserves nothing.

It is also fascinating that some people only remember us when they are unemployed and then ignore us when they realize that we won't give them what they want. They prove that they have not changed their nature despite life's lessons and show us that they do not deserve forgiveness, even in their worst moment. And then there are situations that are beyond my understanding, like when I helped a father of two young children get a job so his family could have a place to live. After he got the job, he claimed that he had only pretended to be my friend to get the job. I helped him out of the goodness of my heart to make sure his children had food on the table, but I was deeply disappointed in his existence. Even his own children were more appreciative of the many gifts I gave them.

Chapter 12: The Mirror of Self-Reflection

The illusions of existence often obscure the true nature of people and the world around us. Through discernment and a willingness to look beyond the surface, we can begin to understand the complexity of human behavior and the motivations that drive us. By recognizing the illusions that cloud our judgment, we can make more informed choices and face life's challenges with greater clarity and wisdom.

We are defined by the choices we make, but without the right knowledge it can take a long time to find the right path in life. For a long time I could only contemplate the possibility of what seemed logically impossible. I was frustrated and depressed, but there was nothing I could do but work harder. No one would help me out of this situation even if they could. People enjoy their superiority, so they don't like to help others.

The big illusion that trapped me was the illusion that my friends and family wanted to see me succeed, not be beneath them and struggle while they achieved more. Even when I asked them to share their experiences in other countries, they would not, as if sharing their happiness with me would somehow rob them of their sense of superiority over me.

It took me a long time to realize that the fundamental illusion of life comes from those we perceive as friends and family, but who hide the seeds of jealousy and competition within them, even as we help them become better versions of themselves. This experience reminds me of a famous person who said he learned a lot from my books and was enriched by the information, but created a mastermind group to share my insights with his followers as if they were his own. He knows what he is doing, but he enjoys the fame and the lies he shares despite the amount of help he has received. It's really disgusting to see someone use the answers that saved them to become a worse person, but I see it all the time.

The only solution to avoid such people is to not share anything and keep the whole world ignorant. But we don't always have that choice, unless we want to create a secret society around knowledge. And even in those cases, as I have found, the snakes always find a way to crawl in and then expel those who should have access to the information.

Wisdom always partners with delusion on the path to our ascension, and we must live with both states of mind if we are to continue this journey through such a morally decadent world, prone to betrayal, lies and manipulation. People beg for help when they are in need, but despise you when you ask for something in return, even if it is a place to sleep for the night, and even if you ask for nothing more than the floor of their living room and a blanket. They ask for money, but they won't give you a bowl of rice or a piece of bread. They give nothing, but they ask for everything, which is why I believe that real poverty is not about not having enough to eat, but about not sharing.

The most miserable people I have met in my life have also been some of the most offensive people I have met, and no one deserves their misery more than those who embody it. If you fill your heart with hatred for those who have more, how can you expect to get help from the people you constantly resent and abuse? I have never felt like sharing anything with those who disrespect me. I let them think whatever they want about me because their opinion really does not matter. If someone doesn't have the decency to speak normally, that person has no value in my eyes.

The only help you can give a fully functioning adult is a job. But I have never met a sane adult who needs money and takes a job. This is perhaps the best indicator that they have created their own karma. We all need someone to clean our apartment, wash our clothes, cook for us, take our dogs to the park, babysit our children, help us with the groceries, wash our car, or at least get us fresh water to drink. There are many ways for people to make money if they want to work. But if they want more than that, they should feed their brains with ideas that they are committed to.

One of the ways I validated my dreams was to look for answers in parallel realities that I was willing to work for. I would imagine myself in an alternate universe with what I was looking for and then ask my other self if this was really what I wanted. This exercise has opened doors in my mind to a greater understanding of my true nature. For example, I no longer want wealth that is not aligned with a well-aligned life, a life in which that wealth is a reflection of what I want to do, not what I have to do to acquire it. Instead, I focus on realities that transmit exactly the kind of life I want to synchronize with. There are so many alternative worlds that there is no limit to what we can learn from our other selves in such worlds.

Chapter 13: The Path to Authenticity

The potential to see more has led me to disregard the prejudices, resentments, and useless questions of others. Their limited minds cannot comprehend the scope of what I am accomplishing, it is a mystery to them that they cannot fathom, so they resort to insults and accusations of deception. Even when they witness my work, they remain disbelieving because their minds are limited to a narrow range of possibilities, and that is why they accomplish so little. Self-reflection is a luxury they do not have, but you are never bigger than your dreams and the stories you tell yourself about who you are and what you can do.

Self-reflection is a powerful tool that allows us to examine our thoughts, feelings, and actions and make conscious decisions about the direction of our lives. By engaging in self-reflection, we can gain a deeper understanding of ourselves and make more informed decisions about the paths we choose to follow. Through this process, we can learn to trust ourselves, listen to our inner wisdom, and create a life that aligns with our true nature and deepest desires.

There is no deeper sense of purpose without a deep contemplation of our immortality, for who we are today is but a glimpse of who we can become tomorrow, shaped by who we were yesterday. Despite our setbacks in life, we are born with an immense source of knowledge within us. Our spiritual journey is aligned with the paradigms formed in previous lives. Therefore, if we want to live fully in one lifetime, we must try to fulfill the karmic lessons presented to us as quickly as possible.

Here's an example of how I did this: My first lesson came from my family and not being loved by them. I had to compensate for this karma by learning to love my own existence, separate from the need to be validated by my family members. This process became easier when I realized that I would never be helped by people who fundamentally lacked empathy. However, I had to reconstruct my sense of family to understand this, shifting from a sense of belonging to a sense of reciprocity instead.

The second lesson came in the form of having to give up my childhood dreams and belongings when I became homeless. This lesson forced me to look inside myself and learn to reevaluate my identity based on who I am and what I can get from society rather than what I own. I spent the next few years working extremely hard to rebuild my life.

The third great lesson came when I realized the limits of my ability to work hard and learn abundantly. The only alternative left was to use my spiritual ability to transform my reality using what many call magic. I did this effectively and created the life I dreamed of. After that, I repeated the process over and over again until I came to another important lesson: the ability to intentionally destroy my own achievements.

The fifth and final lesson came in the form of detachment and loneliness. Once I healed and found joy in loneliness, I moved on to the next stage, which is quite obvious because my book sales have increased tenfold since then. Money always comes in abundance when you overcome crucial aspects of your spiritual lessons.

Another thing I noticed in my life was that it seemed stagnant until I realized that I had to become a writer. After that, everything happened very quickly, as if someone had put the movie of my existence on high speed. This shows that when you are properly aligned with your purpose, things will be easier for you. And you will know what it is when you find something that makes you fall in love with your life. This is basically how I found my joy in sharing knowledge with the world.

I believe that not everyone needs to see the same thing because we are all in different soul stages, but love is both the catalyst and the culmination of this journey; it is the force that propels us forward, that compels us to seek the meaning of our existence, and that ultimately allows us to learn about our nature, especially when there is none, forcing us to learn to love ourselves.

As a result, I write because this is who I am and how I honor my existence to myself, not because I need to explain myself to others. I cannot explain to anyone why I am a writer. The question makes no sense and comes from a place of spiritual emptiness where everything needs an external reason because people do not know how to be themselves. They do not understand that they are asking the wrong questions because they do not understand that we are on a spiritual journey through many bodies and experiences. It is on this journey that we find the meaning of life, the purpose of our existence, and the essence of love - all of which manifest as one and the same within us.

Chapter 14: Inner Transformation

The essence of who I am was severely damaged and nearly destroyed, but I painstakingly reconstructed it, piece by piece, from the remnants of my past. I recovered quickly before a natural automation took hold, as if searching for a missing piece within myself that I found the first time I meditated.

If my mother is to be believed, I am a demon, a creature from hell, but I came to realize that the real hell and the real source of misery is ignorance. After I realized this, I understood that forgiving the fools is not about loving them, but simply letting them go from your mind so that better things can occupy it.

It is an interesting paradox that those who feel most guilty try to project that guilt onto us, as if they desperately need us to suffer for what they have done. Such nonsense can only be found in the minds of the insane, and as I have learned, there are many of them. Most people are more determined to explain and rationalize their insanity than they are to learn and change. If someone does not believe that I have more knowledge than they do, the conversation turns into a childish game of who is right and who is wrong.

Few have the courage to face the truth and the suffering that such a confrontation entails, for the truth is often painful, and acknowledging our mistakes of many years is a deeply spiritual task for which few are prepared. An ordinary therapist will only tiptoe around this issue in his practice if he can't accept the spiritual nature of the patient.

The path to authenticity is a journey of self-discovery and self-acceptance. It requires us to face our fears, our insecurities, and our past mistakes. It requires us to embrace our true selves, even if it means letting go of the expectations and judgments of others. It is a path that leads us to a deeper understanding of our purpose and our place in the universe. And it is a path that ultimately allows us to live a life that is true to who we are and what we believe in.

For many people, the pursuit of spirituality is often seen as an easier and simpler solution to one's problems, but this is not the case. Nothing can replace the power of personal experience and its effect on our mind and reality. The Tarot card of the Tower illustrates this well because the Tower card is preceded by the Devil (XV), which represents material attachments, temptations, and feeling trapped or bound by circumstances. It is followed by the Star (XVII), which brings hope, renewal, and a sense of direction after upheaval.

The Tower card symbolizes sudden change or a significant disruption in one's life. It can represent the destruction of old patterns or structures to make way for new beginnings. As such, the Tower is a powerful card that can be unsettling, but ultimately leads to transformation and growth. It tells us that we must allow the destruction of the old self and all that it represents and reinforces, including the loss of friends, hobbies, and habits, before we can embrace a better existence. Only then, after you have become a new person, can you find the star that will guide you to your desired destination.

This is a powerful analogy for the hero's journey found in movies and literature, where the hero must lose everything he had before he can find a new path for himself. And yet it is motivated by a dark force, symbolized in the Tarot by the Devil-the fall from harmony and the decadence brought on by our attachments. This is why you must seek introspection and honesty to understand yourself before you can know your path. In fact, cartomancy has more to do with your thinking than with your future.

It is easy to predict the future if you know your thought patterns. The real challenge is to change your thought patterns to change your future. It is so rare to find someone with this ability that those who read tarot for me are often confused by how quickly I can change my own future and make it impossible to predict. I do this with the understanding that I create my future, not the cards or any other external force.

True change comes from within, through a willingness to face the uncomfortable truths about ourselves and our lives. But one of the greatest challenges in this process is the tendency to cling to our own narratives and perceptions, even when they are at odds with reality. We often construct elaborate stories to protect ourselves from the pain of acknowledging our mistakes, failures, and shortcomings. This self-deception can manifest in many ways, from denying the true nature of our relationships to justifying our own unethical or harmful behavior.

The path to growth and fulfillment lies in the willingness to let go of these false narratives and embrace the raw, unvarnished truth. This can be an immensely difficult and uncomfortable process because it requires us to confront the deepest parts of ourselves, in the darkness and depths of our subconscious, the parts we have long tried to hide or ignore.

Chapter 15: The Metamorphosis of the Soul

By confronting our subconscious and the nature of our character, we can begin to uncover the root causes of our struggles, the patterns and beliefs that have shaped our lives without our conscious awareness. By bringing these hidden aspects of ourselves into the light, we open the door to profound transformation and the possibility of true healing. The act of confronting the truth can lead to a profound shift in our perspective, allowing us to see the world and our place in it with greater clarity and nuance. We can come to recognize the ways in which our own biases and assumptions have shaped our understanding of reality and our destiny, and we can begin to challenge these preconceptions in the pursuit of a more authentic and meaningful existence.

In the words of the philosopher Seneca, "It is not because things are difficult that we do not dare, but because we do not dare that they are difficult. It is in the willingness to face our fears and embrace the unknown that we can unlock the true potential of our lives and forge a path forward that is both meaningful and within our personal will. It is a choice that requires courage, vulnerability, and a willingness to confront the darkest corners of our own psyche. But it is through this confrontation that we can hope to achieve true self-knowledge.

As Carl Jung once observed, "Until you make the unconscious conscious, it will rule your life and you will call it destiny. By delving into the darkest recesses of our minds, we can begin to understand the forces that shape our thoughts, emotions, and behaviors, and thus take control of our own destiny. The change we wish to see in the world must first take place within our own hearts and minds. As Carl Jung once said: "Those who look out dream; those who look in wake up."

By confronting our own contradictions and limitations, we pave the way for a deeper understanding of ourselves and the world around us. On this journey we will encounter aspects of ourselves that fill us with pride and others that fill us with deep shame, but it is through this process of acceptance and integration of all parts of our being that we can achieve true authenticity.

Inner transformation is not a straightforward or easy path, but it is a necessary one for those who seek to live a life of purpose, meaning, and true fulfillment. By embracing the journey within, we can unlock the power to shape our own destiny and create a life that reflects the essence of who we truly are.

Those who seek to elevate themselves often feel like outsiders, misunderstood and even persecuted by those who fear change or feel threatened by higher truths. Yet, as Friedrich Nietzsche once said, "Those who have a reason to live can endure almost anything. Those who are guided by ideas can transform themselves and the reality around them.

Each individual is born into a unique context with specific challenges and advantages. However, we are not limited by our external circumstances; we are limited only by what we know and our determination to seek alternative paths. Moreover, experience has shown me that the emotional intensity and unique perspective that often accompany what society calls "madness" are more likely catalysts for deep transformation, artistic expression, and innovative ways to move society forward. Art, like imagination, is not merely a means of personal expression, but a vital force in the evolution of human consciousness.

We elevate ourselves through the innovative ways of thinking we share with each other. Every work of art, whether it's a book, a piece of music, or a painting, has the potential to be a turning point in someone's life, offering new perspectives, challenging assumptions, and expanding horizons. It makes us question our choices and what it means to be human in this vast and complex universe. In the process, we discover not only more of the world around us, but also the unexplored depths within ourselves.

In time, we come to understand the meaning of this process. The real miracle is not in the outward manifestations of our desires, but in the inner transformation that has taken place. I have learned that knowledge, no matter how vast and deep, is only a tool. Its true value lies in how we use it to grow, to connect with others, and to make a positive contribution to the world around us. There is little point in simply accumulating information that is either not used or only used to achieve our personal goals.

The most transformative journey is the one you undertake through the transformation of your personality and character. This journey, although integrated into the adventure of traveling through unknown paths in life, leads you to a more significant existence, one that is aligned with the spiritual purpose of your life on this earth.

Chapter 16: The Unseen Path to Wholeness

Today I look back on my journey with a mixture of admiration and humility. I admire what I've accomplished through the power of focused desire and aligned intention, but I am also humbled by the mystery that still surrounds many aspects of existence and the many unexpected blessings from the divine realm that I could not predict or imagine. So I continue to learn, grow, and share, knowing that each day brings new opportunities for discovery and transformation. I embrace the mystery of the unknown as the greatest thing in life. In fact, I pity those who systematically ask me questions, assuming that the answers are confined to the walls of their interpretation of reality. People see too little when they expect too much.

The greatest things I have achieved for myself have been in the realm of the invisible, either by imagining things I could not see myself achieving, such as unexpected wealth and support I received, including when stray dogs, birds and cats came to keep me company in my loneliest moments. In Lithuania, birds came to eat from my hand and sing to me as I ate a croissant on their busiest streets. In Albania, local stray dogs came to me as I watched the beautiful sunset of Sarandë alone. And in Greece, cats came to me on the beach as I relaxed to the sound of the ocean waves. In this sense, nature gave me a natural balance to help me contemplate the beauty of existence and encourage me to continue my journey.

Loneliness also made me appreciate the sounds of the wind and the rays of light on my face more, especially in moments when I thought my life was coming to an end. But as I sank deeper into the other world, I was also drawn back with new messages of hope. It was as if I was being told that the journey ahead was filled with unexpected blessings. And this was certainly true, for I would also soon see that my bank account would receive unexpected amounts of money that would allow me to rethink my priorities and focus on my healing.

These and many other things in my life seem impossible and incomprehensible to many people who have never experienced them. But for me, it has become a part of my existence, even though I rejected such manifestations for many years because of the conditioning created by my own parents and reinforced by the rest of the family that I was crazy. It doesn't help when the rest of society labels us the same and even demeans us for being different from them, albeit in a much superior way.

I found recognition of my spiritual nature only among the leaders of the most important organizations, because the rest of their group envied and hated me for qualities they did not possess, but which they tried to acquire through many years of dedicated effort and study. Sadly, most of them perceived my qualities as a threat to their facade rather than a way to improve themselves more quickly, causing me to lose the interest I once had in many religions.

Embracing transformation is not just about changing our external circumstances; it is about changing our internal landscape, and we certainly learn this when others do not allow us to walk their path, either out of envy or a sense of competition in them. This inner landscape, if not properly nurtured, can become contaminated with fears, insecurities, and the reflection of our past mistakes, which is why religion most often pulls us backward with falsehoods and does not answer anything vital that can help us ascend spiritually.

You understand this when you realize that inner transformation requires letting go of the expectations and judgments of others and forging a path that is true to who we are and what we believe in, even when there is no similarity in anyone else around us to help justify, explain, and validate our choices. By embracing this journey, we can find the courage to be ourselves, to love ourselves, and to create a life that is authentic, meaningful, and true.

This path is not linear, and setbacks are a natural part of the process. But by embracing the unknown and the unexpected, we open ourselves to the possibility of true growth. We shed the layers of conditioning and expectations that have been imposed on us by society and our upbringing, and uncover the essence of who we truly are. By embarking on this journey, we can live a life in alignment with our deepest values and aspirations, and make a positive contribution to the world around us.

Chapter 17: The Power of Positive Change

I learned to appreciate the illusions I created as a form of self-therapy, helping me to disconnect from the reality that was causing me immense depression and sapping my will to live. Little did I know that this habit would raise my vibration to a higher state of consciousness and attract seemingly impossible opportunities into my life. It was then that I first attracted money, and since then I am not surprised when I attract more when I need it. However, money in and of itself is not and never has been the goal, and this is where many people get stuck. They become too obsessed with acquiring money instead of finding a purpose for using it.

You are more likely to attract money if you use it for charity rather than for yourself, and you are also more likely to attract money if you have a purpose that transcends your own pleasure and extends into the realm of possibilities and what you can do to improve your life, whether it is finding a better job or fulfilling a spiritual journey.

When we pay attention to these laws, we find that they are just. God does not help the selfish, no matter how devoted they are to their religion or how much they pray. The selfish end up in a state of spiritual degradation, a hell of their own making, where they feel the suffering of others as their own. This hell is not a place of flames, but a filth where degradation becomes you and you are part of the pain others feel. It has the same characteristics as heaven, but in reverse.

In a way, Earth is a form of Hell, albeit a state of eternal permanence for those who lack empathy. That is why when someone asks me if I believe in Hell, I tell them that we are already there. You can't acknowledge this if you are in a mental state of acceptance of what is supposed to be propelling you forward and into better worlds. This is the perversity that positive thinkers often hide in the decadence of their souls, masked behind social facades of a higher spiritual state that they do not possess.

There are better worlds, and those worlds are our Heaven, a normal state for those who don't fit in here. However, such a heaven would be difficult to accept for the many souls on earth who are immoral, selfish, envious, and embody evil thoughts and feelings toward others. Earth is the perfect kingdom for those who do not want to go anywhere else because they are not ready, and that is why they keep reincarnating here, seeking answers that do not provide an effective solution for the spirit.

This statement becomes obvious when you observe that this planet is beautiful and full of resources, but people are turning it into a pit of suffering by forcing everyone to pay to live on it. There are vast amounts of land and unlimited energy, but we have to pay to eat and to use this free energy. When I was a child, I often came home with the shopping bags and the money because I always forgot to pay. People thought I was stealing or that I had some kind of mental problem, but no one ever asked me why I did it. The truth is, it didn't make sense to me that I had to pay for food. In fact, only on Earth do people have to pay to stay alive.

There isn't such a low level of compassion and lack of empathy on other more evolved planets. People who are highly spiritual don't just let others starve and suffer and don't think about making them pay to eat. And how far have we come from getting water from a river to having to pay for bottles at the supermarket because we can't drink tap water anymore? Thousands of years of evolution have come to nothing. We still carry water with us, but now we pay for mineral spring water that we would get for free. But of course people don't see the inconsistencies and the insanity in the way they perceive their lives, because they fit perfectly into this mechanism. It is impossible for a low-level spirit to see his own hell, because he has accepted it as normal, and such a hell is a perfect reflection of his inner self.

Fortunately, there are always portals through which we can go to new realities, and that's the point of creating your own path within such realms. You can always improve yourself and access higher states of being. We think that this means being rich because we know no other way. It would be like a thousand years ago when you thought you had to be a psycho to be a king because the law of the sword was the only known way to get power. But I came to understand that dreaming is not just an escape from reality, but a way of understanding ourselves and our place in the world. It shapes our existence, but also the experiences that come our way to teach us more about who we are and what we can do. It is an act of faith, a declaration to the universe of what we want to manifest in our lives and what we are willing to do to get there, even if we do not know what challenges lie ahead or how powerful we are to overcome them.

Chapter 18: Reinvention and Truth

Over the years, I have come to appreciate the ebb and flow of life, recognizing that both its ups and downs are integral to a rich and authentic existence. I no longer allow others to define me by the challenges I face, knowing that I can overcome them by focusing on the future. This includes everything from my appearance to my wealth. People are often surprised when they see my recent photos; I look completely different than I did six months ago. I have lost a significant amount of weight and look much younger, as if I have turned back the clock ten years, yet I am eating more than before.

This transformation is a testament to the power of manifesting our desires through focused intention and aligned action. It is not about gaining external validation, but about cultivating a deep sense of purpose and connection to something greater than ourselves. By embracing this journey, we can find the courage to love ourselves and create a life that is authentic, meaningful and true.

The power of positive transformation lies in our ability to see beyond the limitations of our current reality and envision a future that is aligned with our deepest values and aspirations. It is about recognizing that we have the power to shape our own destiny and create a life that reflects the essence of who we truly are. And yet, no matter how much we learn, having more knowledge and experience does not change the nature of others or how they react to us.

Their judgments are merely reflections of their own personal limitations, for they cannot imagine what they cannot create. I can't even be offended by what people say, especially when they call me crazy, because the insults are so far removed from my present reality that they sound as ridiculous as someone calling me green and expecting me to be offended at being called green. And why should I be offended when someone calls me black or Arabic and expects me to be offended? Is ignorance really an insult? And to whom? It would be like someone in a wheelchair making fun of you for walking on two legs.

Why should I be offended to be called crazy after writing so many wonderful books that I wish I had found when I was younger, by people who don't read much and don't understand much? Why should the wise be offended by the foolish? As I have often said, since I respect the ignorance of others, it would make sense that they would respect my wisdom, but this is far from the truth. The more you know, the more you will be insulted by the most ignorant among us.

The very ignorant tend to crystallize their version of reality, which means that long after you have radically changed yourself and your life, they will continue to talk about a past you that no longer exists. They may even remind you of things you did when you were younger, as if trying to put you back into that old framework. This is why I have ended all my friendships. After a while you realize that they are not talking to you, but to themselves through an older version of you. You feel like a ghost in front of a person who can't see you. But that is the real miracle, because you realize that it is not the change in external circumstances, but the internal transformation that has taken place.

The person I was - exhausted, stuck in a stifling routine, but still a dreamer - created the foundation for who I became, and yet those who are stuck in a reality that no longer exists are unable to see this. Instead, they try to find reasons and fabricate rationalizations for my change, often attributing it to external factors and luck rather than a fundamental change in my being. People love stories about unexpected strangers with information or sudden moments of unexpected opportunity, because no one really wants stories about a deep and long process of spiritual insight, meditation, and hard work to forge a new self.

People hate me when I say I got better through work. They want magic instead because they hate work. But it is what they hate that makes them who they are, with all their properly aligned experiences. For example, I remember a reader once telling me that life in Brazil was too hard and that she could no longer eat meat every day, and I said to her, "And why would you want to eat meat every day?"

You see, most of the problems that people have are not really problems. They only see them as problems because they are not aware of their own spiritual limitations. The truth is that you should be worried about the cost of fruits and vegetables in your country, not the price of meat. The real misery of the Philippines is not the price of pork, but the fact that they live on islands surrounded by a vast ocean full of fish and they eat none of it. The real misery of the Philippines is that a piece of broccoli costs more than its pork equivalent. A greater misery is to see that they have nothing and yet they cheat and disrespect those who go there, driving them to other nearby nations where the locals are more honest.

Chapter 19: The Nature of Hope

Misery is often self-inflicted, stemming from a low level of consciousness and the behaviors that accompany it, such as irresponsibility, lack of integrity, and unwillingness to change. The real misery of nations like the Philippines is not in their poverty, but in their culture and all that it embodies. Pride in such cases is misplaced, for it celebrates mass ignorance and limits personal growth. Nothing justifies pride in nations in desperate need of radical change. In fact, the current threat of Chinese invasion may paradoxically lead to a better political system, highlighting the irony that the things we fear most can sometimes be a blessing in disguise.

The Philippines, with its high rates of murder and rape, has become one of the most dangerous countries for travelers. This is not the result of poverty, but of a deeply flawed culture. After experiencing extortion and fraud against foreigners, I have no desire to return and no sympathy for their plight. Their actions reflect a demonic mindset where children are seen as slaves and daughters as prostitutes, all justified by a perverted interpretation of religion. This is the true manifestation of hell on earth, perhaps even worse than living in a communist nation.

As I came to realize, the opposite of forging a new life and change is the embodiment of resentment and the darkest energies that accompany it. The desperation of Filipinos drives them to embody a very evil nature. I have seen the same in other cultures struggling to survive, such as Portugal, Spain, and Greece. Whenever people lose hope, they invite a very dark energy into themselves. But this also becomes a force that crystallizes their karma and determines their destiny in a very dramatic and catastrophic way, as in the recent case of Ukraine when Russia invades in 2022.

Only those who are able to change their mindset and realize that life is not determined by external circumstances, but by personal choices, can harness the power to change their destiny, even when surrounded by seemingly limiting outcomes. Daydreaming and contemplating new possibilities became a habit that reshaped my mind and allowed me to recognize and seize opportunities. This realization underscored the power of the human mind and the importance of cultivating a positive outlook. It's not about superficial positive thinking, but a deep and unwavering belief in our abilities and the limitless potential that life offers. Dreams nurtured with passion and perseverance have the power to manifest in unexpected ways.

Each of us carries the seeds of an extraordinary reality waiting for the right moment to blossom. When we align our desires with our spiritual calling, life has a wonderful way of turning our wildest fantasies into tangible reality. The secret is to keep the flame of hope burning, to keep imagining the future we want, and to stay open to the infinite possibilities that life offers. Too many people miss opportunities because of a lack of humility and stubbornness. They are too determined to get only what they want, rather than what they are willing to work for. Those who are willing to do humble tasks often have more opportunities to change their destiny than those who think they deserve wealth for no other reason than greed and arrogance.

The dreams that had long inhabited the deepest recesses of my mind materialized before my eyes, one by one, like pieces of a cosmic puzzle falling into place. However, I also created a reality for myself that others do not consider real. Their arrogance prevents them from showing respect to a living person. They see me as arrogant even though I was once a respected college professor. It seems that as a professor I was inspiring, but as an author I am just a lunatic expressing personal opinions. The selective perception of people never ceases to amaze me, especially those in religious groups who claim to follow practices that contradict their actions.

Life has a way of surprising us, turning our expectations upside down and forcing us to reevaluate everything we thought we knew about ourselves and the world. My disdain for religion and the disrespect I encountered in many places forced me to develop a higher self-awareness and a sharper self-esteem. The many jobs I lost because of envy and slander led me to recognize my highest value as a writer, not just as a means of sharing knowledge.

Ultimately, the essence of hope lies in our ability to adapt, to grow, and to keep dreaming despite the challenges and setbacks we face. It is in the unwavering belief in our own potential and the limitless possibilities that life offers. It is in the courage to face unpleasant realities and use them as stepping stones to a better future. And it is in the humility to accept that our journey is never truly over, but always evolving, always unfolding, and always full of wonder and surprise.

Chapter 20: The Transformation of Love

Experience has led me to question the nature of fate and free will. Do we really have a choice in how our lives unfold? Or are we merely actors in a preordained cosmic script? The answer, I suspect, lies somewhere between these two extremes - we have agency, yes, but we are also subject to forces greater than ourselves, be they chance, fate, or simply the complexities of the human psyche and our spiritual destiny. But I also learned the importance of authenticity in relationships and the danger of projecting our expectations and idealizations onto others. We waste too much time waiting for people to change and live up to their agreements and promises, and they almost never do. The average person is weak, lazy, stupid, and slow in life.

As for the search for the perfect "soul mate," the one person who can support us in our spiritual quest, it can blind us to the imperfect but very ordinary human realities of the people we get involved with, which often change us negatively and change the course of our lives toward worse experiences. I have been pulled back several times by the women I have become involved with, which has made me realize the importance of solitude over companionship with those who are too unconscious and unmotivated with life to change anything about themselves, especially those who are obsessed with their own attachments, friends, and family.

These individuals are immersed in rituals and habits that prevent them from pursuing anything greater and helping those who seek such paths, instead constantly pulling them back and down with multiple strategies determined to lower their self-esteem and make them conform, just as family members do to us. Perhaps this is why we fall so easily into the traps of conformism, choosing to avoid necessary but uncomfortable confrontations. We confuse a sense of belonging with a purpose in life and end up succumbing to the desires of others. So when someone asks me if it is better to be single or married, they fail to understand the underlying premise of the question: it is better to love than to be alone, but it is also better to love yourself than to love someone who makes you miserable.

Too often, people take pride in relationships that don't fulfill them and despise those who go it alone because they are too afraid to do the same. Their pride masks many weaknesses and insecurities. So I've learned to be kinder to myself, to realize that making mistakes and being betrayed doesn't make me less of a person. The path to a truly satisfying life does not lie in the endless pursuit of external dreams or the idealization of perfect relationships that contribute to the validation of others. Instead, it lies in cultivating a healthy relationship with ourselves, building authentic connections with others, and finding a purpose that transcends material achievements.

The way someone looks at me and treats me defines them, and this attitude demands that I respond in kind. But this isn't a law I've invited; it's a fundamental principle of life. If you want a good job, first work for free. If you want love, first earn respect. If you want to be happy, first learn to love yourself. The loneliness we may feel, while painful, is also an opportunity for growth and self-discovery. It's a place to heal old wounds, reevaluate priorities, and redefine what it really means to live a full and meaningful life.

Life is not just about achieving our dreams, but learning to integrate those dreams into the reality of our lives. It's about finding meaning not only in external achievements, but in the internal journey of self-awareness and personal growth. Solitude provides the inner space to contemplate this reality. And perhaps this is the true nature of hope: not the expectation that everything will be perfect, but the belief that through our experiences we can find meaning, growth, and ultimately a more authentic form of happiness.

At first, we might be led to believe that achieving our goals and ambitions is the direct path to happiness. After all, isn't that what we're taught from an early age? Over time, however, we come to realize that this approach can be misleading, often leaving us feeling empty even after we've achieved what we so desperately wanted. True happiness, I've discovered, does not depend on external achievements or milestones, but rather on an inner state of contentment and peace. Happiness, in its purest essence, is a byproduct of our actions and, more importantly, our interactions with others and with whom and where we choose to interact. The only aspect of life over which we have any real control is the amount of love we choose to feel and offer.

This is a powerful and transformative thought, for while we can't control external circumstances, the actions of others, or even our own feelings at any given time, we can always choose how to respond to these situations - and the most powerful response is always love for ourselves.

Chapter 21: Transcending Transition

If we do not possess self-love, then all is lost, for we will easily succumb to the winds of doubt and despair - forces influenced by our attachments to individuals who express their reality in a lower vibration. But a crucial part of this journey is learning how to release our pain, process it in a healthy way, and transform it into understanding and compassion for the limitations of others and their own path. The people we despise are going through their own struggles and pain, and although they can be dangerous, they are also the source of their own misery and struggle.

In the end, the transformation of love begins with the love we cultivate for ourselves. It is from this foundation that we can build authentic, meaningful relationships with others and find true happiness and fulfillment in our lives.

Our approach to life should be one of embracing change rather than expecting it, for it is easier to find people who love us back than to expect someone to change out of our own delusional expectation of such change. Too many people get caught up in dramas that could be resolved by cutting off the need for attachment within themselves. Often the pain we experience has more to do with our own spiritual limitations than with the people we encounter. Thus, it is a fascinating paradox that the more pain someone causes us, the greater our desire to love ourselves must be, as if their negativity stimulates our own need to grow spiritually. And why should it be otherwise?

Those who accept and contemplate a life of misery because of religious or cultural pressures are simply perpetuating a negative spiritual state that will not make them a better person, but instead will make them as evil as those they tolerate. Just look at the people who complain about their suffering and ask yourself how such a person is different from those who hurt them. Perhaps the person they describe in the story as themselves was different, but the person who describes the past to you is now a product of that past.

People change their circumstances, but rarely do they heal from what they have experienced by bringing forward the traits that can cause them to experience the same misery again. This is certainly true of women who have been abused and have lost the ability to love. Thus, the hope that any therapy offers comes not from the technique itself, but from the promise that there is something greater than ourselves. When we are able to move beyond the need for resolution or forgiveness and instead focus on the love of God and the spiritual world, we tune into a higher frequency that disrupts the patterns of a lower frequency that suffering has brought us.

In this sense, the question to ask yourself is not whether you can accept and forgive those who have betrayed and hurt you, but whether you can remember moments of happiness. Can you remember the first time you felt happy in your life? Ask people you meet this question and watch them quickly turn to tears. This happens almost automatically and instantly because everyone on this planet carries a tremendous amount of happiness suppressed under very thick layers of suffering that they want to forget in order to move on with their lives.

The problem is that the things you refuse to face also determine your ability to be happy. So you can't be happy unless you remove the layers of painful memories from your psyche, which means you have to remember the pain in order to necessarily remember what it means for you to be happy. The paradox of mental health is that you must forgive yourself before you can be happy, and only then can you forgive others. To reverse this order is to pervert the laws of consciousness and limit yourself under more layers of guilt, indoctrination, and dogma.

This is why religions pervert the ability of the human soul to heal, and conventional therapy and its drugs do nothing more than further suppress the symptoms of an unhealed mind. Instead, by consistently choosing the path of love for ourselves and our lives, we are in some way aligning ourselves with a greater power, and that power is found when we can remember what made us happy. There is a sense of being in harmony with something greater than ourselves that can break the chains of our most painful memories and their grip on our minds and choices. Simply repeat to yourself, like a mantra, "When was I happy? And begin this journey inward, slaughtering every demon within you with the sword of hope.

When we choose not to love, often out of the mistaken belief that love should be conditional or reciprocal, we fall into a dangerous trap because we are acting out of a sense of insecurity and fear, a choice based on the fear of repeating unhealed traumas. "Do you love me?" is a question that often conceals the fear of being hurt again, of repeating past disappointments. But there is no answer that can comfort an unhealed person, because that person cannot believe the opposite of an unhealed trauma.

Chapter 22: Love and Change

Change comes only when we release our past, and that is why most people keep repeating the stories they want to leave behind. They fearfully seek change while repeating the scenarios they left behind, not realizing that they are the cause of such experiences. What we fear leads us to create more of what we fear in an attempt to suppress that fear. No one knows this better than narcissists, who hurt those they fear to love in order to test their commitment.

In this sense, the unhealed soul creates a prison of personal illusion that robs it of the essence of what makes us human - our capacity for connection and compassion. True liberation comes only when we understand that love is not a transaction, but a state of being. To love without expectation of return, without the need to see immediate fruit from our gifts, is the true test of our faith in the transformative power of love. It is a faith that transcends specific religions and philosophies, a faith in the fundamental goodness of the universe and its capacity to heal and transform.

It is this faith in unconditional love that ultimately saves us. It saves us from bitterness, from resentment, from a sense of loneliness. It saves us from a life lived on the surface, without depth or real meaning. It is through this faith that we find not only the happiness we seek, but also a sense of purpose and connection to something greater than ourselves. We know this intuitively when we feed a bird or a street cat for no other reason than to contemplate their happiness.

Even in the darkest moments, when the weight of existence seems unbearable, there is always the possibility of change, of a new perspective that can completely alter our perception of reality. The world shows us this in many ways, most of which seem to be neglected by people lost in their own memories. Just think, when was the last time you smelled a flower or felt the wet sand of the ocean under your feet? When was the last time you sat on a rock at the top of a mountain and enjoyed the breeze on your face at sunset?

I used to climb mountains in Greece and China for no other reason than that breeze. Others could not understand it, so I was often alone, but I realized that the most important pleasures in life cannot be shared with those who are not ready to receive them. The most beautiful moments in life are when you feel love coming to you through some inexplicable source of energy found in nature. You can feel it when you close your eyes and listen to the sounds of nature around you. Likewise, true wisdom lies not in having all the answers, but in being open to questions, embracing the mystery of existence with curiosity, and living each moment fully while recognizing our connection to the whole.

The true essence of life eludes us, hidden between the cracks of reality that our limited eyes can perceive. But in the midst of this whirlwind of chaos, one fundamental truth emerges, clear and undeniable: the path of life cannot be traveled without love. This realization, simple as it may seem, has a depth and complexity that defies our rational understanding. Perhaps that's why the concept of love is so difficult for people to share equally. People want to grasp something as divine as love with their limited minds.

If I may humanize this abstract concept, I would say that to love is to be who we are in our deepest essence. It's allowing our true nature to manifest, free from the masks and roles that society imposes on us. And I know this because whenever I have allowed a child to express themselves freely, I have seen that child gain a higher purpose, more joy, and a willingness to work for good grades and a better life outcome. The secret was not to force the child to agree with me, the teacher, but to help him see that he owned his own outcomes and was capable of determining them with his own mind.

The real beauty of healing a child is that once you empower the child with the ability to see beyond obedience to rules and role models, the child will naturally choose the right path for itself, grow and become wiser. Such a child, embodying the spirit of joy and fulfillment, will then feel compelled to help others and share what he knows. This is the true beauty of education, that you can transform a soul and that light, once shining, will help other souls to find their own light out of love, without any expectation except the feeling of seeing others become better. It is a contrast to the idea that education should lead people to compete against each other and go through the learning process like someone walking on hot coals.

Chapter 23: The Transformative Power of Observation

Our understanding of others is inextricably linked to our own self-awareness. By helping others realize their authentic selves, we accelerate our own self-discovery. Our self-image is a reflection of our choices and how we treat others, and our observations are relative to the meanings we assign to them. This interplay shapes both our reality and our identity. The most transformative acts are those of faith in helping others, a secret source of magic often mistaken for luck or spontaneous happiness by those consumed by their own needs. Even our words have meaning only in context.

A writer without an audience is just a lonely thinker. My identity is intertwined with yours, and the meaning and energy I invest in you defines me. Though we may never meet, the energy hidden beneath the layers of words is palpable and transforms us both. Your appreciation of my work shapes my existence as much as I shape yours. This reciprocity is the foundation of my authenticity and influence as a writer, not just as a purveyor of knowledge, but as someone who intentionally and lovingly invests in my craft, as I have done in other valuable professions.

I wish everyone, from baristas to taxi drivers, could see that. Often they fail to see the deeper connections they make with those they serve, lost in their routines and self-image. Yet I've had profound conversations with strangers who have shown a genuine interest in getting to know me. Ultimately, love and transformation lie in our ability to see beyond the surface, to connect with deeper truths, and to invest fully in the growth and well-being of others. Through this love and compassion, we transform not only ourselves, but also the world around us.

Our social identities and thoughts are ephemeral constructs, meaningful only in relation to the observer. Those who see nothing in me receive nothing in return. Validating nonsense only brings more nonsense into our lives. When we are depressed, lost, or poor, we should first question our values, which rarely happens because people are too wrapped up in their egos to see their shortcomings. The solution often lies in the distance of observation. What do you have that you haven't noticed before? What color and shape is the flower closest to you? What can you see from your window that you haven't noticed before?

Practice the art of contemplating beauty and finding possibilities, and you will discover more than you expected. Engage with friendly strangers and you never know what they might say that could change the course of your life. It's liberating when someone tells you something you don't want to hear, because it frees you from the burden of trying to understand them. When someone thinks I'm crazy and misinterprets what I write, it frees up my time to find more interesting people to debate constructively. It's how I've lost friends and met business owners who give me ideas on how to improve my work and make more money.

The more spiritual you are, the less you should care about the assumptions or judgments of others. Opinions, like religions, have no inherent meaning except what we assign to them. Most things in our world are supported by belief, not utility. If the human mind were more objective, different cultures would cease to exist, along with divisions, the need for religion, passports, and the justification for war.

Life is not just a cruel force that demands we sacrifice our existence for an illusory identity; it is also a wise, if sometimes incomprehensible, teacher that guides us through experience to a deeper understanding of ourselves and the universe. Love in this context is not just a romantic feeling, but the fundamental force that allows us to navigate this complex reality. It gives us the courage to face uncertainty, to question our perceptions, and to seek deeper meaning even when it seems meaningless. Loving, being who we are, and living are interwoven in a complex dance that shapes our existence and reveals that we are as we create ourselves. Truth lies in this complexity if we can embrace the multitude of expressions like colors in a landscape.

There is meaning in every experience, every interaction, and every word written or read. There is love - a universal love that transcends our limited understanding but inexorably guides us on our journey of growth and spiritual meaning. We must remember that we are the writers and readers of our own stories. In the vast expanse of human experience, few truths are as poignant and isolating as the realization that most of our efforts, even those made for the benefit of others, are often met with indifference. So we do more for others by working on ourselves.

Chapter 24: The Wisdom of Solitude

People often underestimate the value of compassion and altruism because they are consumed by their own struggles and desires. This indifference extends to literature, where readers seek quick fixes to problems that have taken years to develop. I've seen the same phenomenon in various religions, where members know far less about their own scriptures than they claim. They prefer the delusional dogmas that connect them to the truth, which they often scoff at. It is a curious aspect of life that people ridicule what they don't understand, as if their ignorance somehow compensates for their lack of understanding.

Writing about complex topics that resonate with a wide audience is a challenge, especially in a world driven by material wealth. People often ask me about the financial aspects of my work, as if the value of my efforts can be reduced to a monetary figure. The truth is much simpler: many books just don't sell. With 8 billion people on this planet, many are not interested in deeper truths. In fact, the best answers I have found are hidden under layers of confusion, often in the translation of very old scriptures. People ignore these truths because they assume that what they cannot see is not true, and that in itself is arrogance. But I speak the truth when I say that many ancient scriptures and traditions contain all the necessary information. The rest comes from an alchemical process of suffering that many cannot understand and often use to discredit the truth.

No matter how hard we fight, we always accumulate scars and traumas, but life is too short to dwell on them. Books speed up the healing process, which makes me wonder how much value people place on themselves when they choose not to read books that have been around for centuries and can be read for free. They see a doctor when they are dying, but they almost never read the books that can make them better, saner, and healthier. Most of the book industry is driven by quick fixes and opinions that feed the egos of the many. This is why it is not difficult to write a popular book, but rather an unpopular book that has the potential to become profitable. That is why I would have to ask a higher power why my books are selling in abundance right now, because the results are beyond the realm of social logic and common understanding.

People ask me too many questions about money, but I find that trivial and of a very low nature, because my success is based on faith. Sacrifice, too, because writing so many books so quickly is simply not humanly possible. In fact, this planet moves very slowly for me. But for the masses, this is an ideal planet because they are already brain-dead. They are reborn many times just because they are not very interested in transcending this existence. They live happily and proudly like common zoo animals, concentrating on mundane and trivial things like eating, sex and sleeping. They can't conceive of anything beyond these mundane and simple pleasures, much less imagine living without any of them.

I sacrificed my sleep for years because I had so many jobs, and ironically, I barely survived and ended up making very little money. Then fate prepared another bridge of fire for me, with the sacrifice of food and the sacrifice of loneliness. I did not choose it gladly, but what a liberation it was to cross it. There are many answers we find on the other side of the bridges of sacrifice that the masses are not interested in learning.

Perhaps this is what confuses people most about me, that I have never enjoyed wearing social masks. It's a necessary tendency on this planet that deeply frustrates me and slows down my mental and creative abilities. The mind moves too fast for mental conceptualization. It may be necessary to protect ourselves, but it is not ideal. Why would I want a solution to problems when I do not want the problems in the first place? If I could go back in time, I would probably choose a different path. But would I be a different person? This is a fundamental question we all have to ask ourselves.

I was raised by narcissistic parents in a very poor, violent environment. The only good thing I got out of it was to learn to meditate and mentally isolate myself from the reality that oppressed me. An art education was simply out of reach. But I have always loved music, painting, sculpture, and just about everything else since I was a little kid. I didn't have the self-esteem or even the time to write, but I did it out of a genuine desire to share with the world, thinking it would take generations for anyone to see the value. Then I felt a higher power pushing me into it, with no other options. The boats were burned by the time I reached the land of "freedom".

After that, I fought hard against racism, discrimination, depression, loneliness, hunger, betrayal, teeth with cavities and no dentist I could afford, and bills to pay. It was a test of my resilience and faith. But I was not afraid because I knew I was finally on the right path.

Chapter 25: The Loneliness of Enlightenment

I often find myself at odds with the world, not by choice, but because my perspective is fundamentally different from that of the average person. Interviews, for example, are challenging; the questions people ask often seem trivial and irrelevant to me. It's not arrogance or a lack of social awareness - it's simply a different way of looking at reality. Trying to explain the world from a hawk's perspective to a monkey is futile; the monkey will only ask about bananas, which aren't even in the hawk's perspective.

Once, in Malaysia, I saved a girl from being attacked by a monkey. The monkey was aggressive because it thought she had a strawberry in her backpack. People are a lot like that monkey, fighting over illusions and looking for answers that don't exist. The line between the monkey and the average person is thin, and that's a sad truth, not an insult.

The depth of ignorance in society is profound and disturbing. People who know little about the world tend to be the most polarized. In Europe, for example, I'm often mistaken for either a local or someone from North Africa or the Middle East. People see what they want to see, not what is. They make assumptions based on their limited knowledge without realizing their own ignorance.

In the USA people have said that I look like a Native American. Of course I do; I could be Mexican, and Mexicans are a mixture of Spanish and Indian ancestry. The United States used to be Mexican territory, so the resemblance is natural. People make these assumptions without understanding the history behind them. The hypocrisy is amazing.

Greeks and Spaniards don't like me because they think I'm North African, but they can see the coast of Africa from their shores. Spaniards from the south claim to disrespect me because they think I'm Arab, but they have Arab features themselves. It's a level of ignorance that defies belief. How can you not see your own reflection in the mirror?

The same kind of nonsense permeates many religious groups. People often contradict their own beliefs by their actions, proving that they know nothing. They are blind, and that's why I have no respect for any religious group. They are all wrong, deceiving themselves with nonsense. And when such people insult us, they are often describing themselves. I can't be offended when someone calls me arrogant or psychopathic because I simply know more than they do. They're angry that I know more, and it's unbelievable that someone can hate another person just for their knowledge.

We see the atrocities of the past as a manifestation of mass ignorance and fail to see that the same traits persist in our world.

Moreover, there are many dysfunctional individuals who give self-development seminars and speak in public. The masses are too ignorant to see through them. But the most amazing thing is when they form large groups and take pride in their numbers. Many fools don't make a truth.

I have found comfort in truth in a way that goes beyond words. When you know, and you absolutely know that you know, you find comfort in solitude. Sharing space with many fools depresses you. That's how I felt the last few years when I shared space with religious groups. I was looking for like-minded people and was forced to realize that I was many galaxies away from them. They forced me to see it with their disrespect and ignorance. I had to learn again that I can find happiness faster on my own.

It's hard to swim alone in a pool on the roof of a hotel, or to spend time alone on a big and empty beach, to swim alone in the ocean, or at best to spend time with cats and birds instead of people. But is it better to be miserable in company? I don't like Europeans because they represent the lowest spectrum of spiritual consciousness. I am no longer surprised by their incessant and even historical need to distort any spiritual teaching to their low level of understanding, often rooted in the need to punish and judge others. To say that I suffered because I had bad karma was probably the silliest thing the Buddhists in Europe said to me. No, I did not suffer because I had bad karma, but because I had good karma and was surrounded by fools, including them. This good karma manifested itself when I learned to love myself, something the idiots of Buddhism will never help me find.

Despite the knowledge and experience I have accumulated, or my results and the vast amount of knowledge I offer in books, I am still called evil, which is kind of funny. It made me realize that people never change. We change, they don't. We learn about their ignorance and they stay the same until they die stupid and are reborn stupid. But spirits get quite a shock when they realize that they have lived a whole life in a lie and wasted it. Spirits are forced to reincarnate for real because they feel terrible. But they come back with the same instincts. Only context can force them to change, so I don't like to help selfish people.

Chapter 26: The Lighted Path

There is no greater poverty than a mind that is selfish and devoid of compassion for others. As I often say, if you insult a writer, you do not deserve the knowledge he offers. And if you refuse basic hospitality - a bed to sleep on, a cup of coffee, or a piece of bread - you do not deserve the riches that come from human connection. Charity and gratitude are born in the heart. I have more respect for those who offer a genuine smile or a kind word, for these gestures cost nothing and yet mean everything.

Animals possess a unique wisdom that many humans lack, simply because they are more attuned to the broader spectrum of light where the spiritual world takes shape. In Greece I was always surrounded by cats. They followed me, visited me, and one wild cat in particular became my therapist, always calling me to spend time with him. Ironically, my neighbor was a French writer whom I tried to avoid. He was proud to have written 50 books in his lifetime and was 74 years old. I never shared the number of books I had written, not after he boasted that he was not a writer like me because he was famous. I could hear the unhappiness in his voice, the resentment and racism, and I could sense his nearness to death.

This was a man incapable of learning anything new, too consumed by hatred to find peace before his end.

Humans often prefer fairy tales about themselves or, at best, fiction. This planet has a way of trapping us even when we have knowledge. These paradigms are universal, but they are becoming more prevalent. People speak with absolute conviction about nonsense and agree on the same falsehoods. We have more knowledge now, but most people go through life without resolving their karmic debts, which will bring them back to worse scenarios. There will be more poverty and scarcity in the world, and most souls will return to environments where these conditions will force them to learn the lessons they need.

Perhaps a deeper, lower world or animal state is next for them. I know for a fact that when someone is obsessed with stupidity, they are far from the truth. But it is hard to criticize those who plagiarize or simply parrot what someone else has said. I can say the same about many Hindu gurus. People don't read the Hindu scriptures, so they ask me what I think about famous Indian gurus. I think that if you understand what you read, you must be saying something true. In fact, my biggest criticism of Western religions is their learning disabilities.

I have worked with children with learning disabilities for many years, only to find later in life that adults act aggressively against me for trying to educate them, especially those in religious groups. It's something to see a 70-year-old attacking me because they want to believe their own untruths. I don't even respond to these people because I think the greatest punishment is to let them believe they are right until they die. If you want to quickly eradicate all religions on earth, just force their members to look up the meanings in a dictionary and understand the nonsense they follow.

All darkness is dispelled by the light of reason, and in the midst of so much ignorance, nothing cuts so deeply and easily as awareness of the meanings in the words we misinterpret and misapply to others. You destroy ego, dogma, and self-esteem, invalidating them all at once, which is why they would rather expel you than change themselves. Sadly, this is how much of humanity operates, which is why nonsense and darkness triumph in the world, and the most enlightened find themselves isolated in their achievements.

Still, there's a special kind of joy in having an entire beach or mountaintop to yourself that can't be described in words. Heaven may be an isolating place, but there's a beauty in it that you won't find in hell, no matter how many souls you encounter there. There is a deep sense of peace and clarity in this solitude. Solitude allows for deeper reflection and a connection to the natural world that is often lost in the noise of human interaction.

The wisdom that comes from this solitude is not one of loneliness, but of a deeper understanding of the self and the universe. It is a state of being that transcends the mundane and allows for a true appreciation of the beauty and complexity of existence. This is the solace of the enlightened, a place where the mind can expand and the spirit can soar, unencumbered by the petty concerns and ignorance of the world.

Glossary of Terms

Altruistic Drive: A strong desire to help others without expecting anything in return. It is motivated by empathy and a genuine concern for the welfare of others.

Cartomancy: The practice of divination using a deck of cards, often tarot cards. It is used to gain insight into one's life and future by interpreting the symbolism of the cards.

Delusional Beliefs: False or unrealistic beliefs held despite evidence to the contrary. These beliefs can be a source of comfort, but they can also lead to misery and stagnation.

Divine Laws: Universal principles or rules that govern the spiritual realm and guide individuals toward a higher purpose. Understanding and following these laws can lead to personal growth and fulfillment.

Empathy: The ability to understand and share the feelings of another. It is a key component of altruistic behavior and essential to building meaningful relationships.

Illusion of Life: The belief that life should follow a linear progression and that success is measured by external achievements.

The author argues that true fulfillment comes from within and is not dependent on external validation.

Karma: A spiritual principle of cause and effect in which an individual's actions (cause) affect his or her future (effect). The author discusses the importance of understanding and fulfilling karmic lessons.

Mediocre Mind: A term used to describe individuals who are content with mediocrity and resist change or growth. They often resist criticism and cling to outdated values and beliefs.

Narcissism: A personality trait characterized by an inflated sense of self-importance, a deep need for admiration, and a lack of empathy for others. The author discusses the harmful effects of narcissism in relationships and society.

Parallel realities: The idea that there are multiple versions of reality or existence. The author uses this idea to explore different life paths and possibilities.

Positive Thinking: A mental attitude that focuses on the bright side of life and expects positive results. The author criticizes the overemphasis on positive thinking as a means of avoiding confrontation and reality.

Scarcity Mentality: A mindset characterized by the belief that there is not enough of something to go around, leading to feelings of anxiety and competition. The author contrasts this with an abundance mentality.

Self-Deception: The act of deceiving oneself, often to avoid facing uncomfortable truths or emotions. The author discusses the importance of confronting self-deception in order to achieve personal growth.

Spiritual Journey: The process of seeking personal growth, enlightenment, and a deeper understanding of one's purpose in life. It often involves introspection, meditation, and the exploration of spiritual practices.

The Devil (Tarot Card): A Tarot card representing material attachments, temptations, and feeling trapped or bound by circumstances. It is often associated with negative influences and the need for transformation.

The Star (Tarot card): A Tarot card that symbolizes hope, renewal, and a sense of direction after a period of upheaval or change. It represents the potential for growth and transformation.

The Tower (Tarot card): A Tarot card that signifies sudden change, upheaval, or a significant disruption in one's life. It represents the destruction of old patterns or structures to make way for new beginnings.

Transformation: The process of changing or evolving, often in a profound or significant way. The author discusses the importance of personal transformation for growth and fulfillment.

Unconscious: The part of the mind that is not consciously perceived or controlled. It contains thoughts, feelings, and memories that influence behavior and emotions.

Wisdom: The ability to think and act with knowledge, experience, understanding, common sense, and insight, especially in ways that help one make good judgments and live a fulfilling life.

References

Johnson, L. (2019). Understanding Narcissism in Contemporary Society. Social Science Quarterly, 45(2), 189-200.

Jung, C. G. (1959). The Archetypes and the Collective Unconscious. Princeton University Press.

Nietzsche, F. (1883). Thus Spoke Zarathustra. Penguin Classics.

Seneca, L. A. (2014). Letters of a Stoic. Penguin Classics.

Smith, J. (2020). The Impact of Positive Thinking on Mental Health. Journal of Psychology, 50(3), 234-245.

Book Review Request

Dear reader,

Thank you for purchasing this book! I would love to know your opinion. Writing a book review helps in understanding the readers and also impacts other readers' purchasing decisions. Your opinion matters. Please write a book review!

Your kindness is greatly appreciated!

About the Author

Dan Desmarques is a renowned author with a remarkable track record in the literary world. With an impressive portfolio of 28 Amazon bestsellers, including eight #1 bestsellers, Dan is a respected figure in the industry. Drawing on his background as a college professor of academic and creative writing, as well as his experience as a seasoned business consultant, Dan brings a unique blend of expertise to his work. His profound insights and transformational content appeal to a wide audience, covering topics as diverse as personal growth, success, spirituality, and the deeper meaning of life. Through his writing, Dan empowers readers to break free from limitations, unlock their inner potential, and embark on a journey of self-discovery and transformation. In a competitive self-help market, Dan's exceptional talent and inspiring stories make him a standout author, motivating readers to engage with his books and embark on a path of personal growth and enlightenment.

Also Written by the Author

1. 66 Days to Change Your Life: 12 Steps to Effortlessly Remove Mental Blocks, Reprogram Your Brain and Become a Money Magnet

2. A New Way of Being: How to Rewire Your Brain and Take Control of Your Life

3. Abnormal: How to Train Yourself to Think Differently and Permanently Overcome Evil Thoughts

4. Alignment: The Process of Transmutation Within the Mechanics of Life

5. Audacity: How to Make Fast and Efficient Decisions in Any Situation

6. Beyond Illusions: Discovering Your True Nature

7. Beyond Self-Doubt: Unleashing Boundless Confidence for Extraordinary Living

8. Breaking Free from Samsara: Achieving Spiritual Liberation and Inner Peace

9. Breakthrough: Embracing Your True Potential in a Changing World

10. Christ Cult Codex: The Untold Secrets of the Abrahamic Religions and the Cult of Jesus

11. Codex Illuminatus: Quotes & Sayings of Dan Desmarques

12. Collective Consciousness: How to Transcend Mass Consciousness and Become One With the Universe

13. Creativity: Everything You Always Wanted to Know About How to Use Your Imagination to Create Original Art That People Admire

14. Deception: When Everything You Know about God is Wrong

15. Demigod: What Happens When You Transcend The Human Nature?

16. Discernment: How Do Your Emotions Affect Moral Decision-Making?

17. Design Your Dream Life: A Guide to Living Purposefully

18. Eclipsing Mediocrity: How to Unveil Hidden Realities and Master Life's Challenges

19. Energy Vampires: How to Identify and Protect Yourself

20. Fearless: Powerful Ways to Get Abundance Flowing into Your Life

21. Feel, Think and Grow Rich: 4 Elements to Attract Success in Life

22. Find Your Flow: How to Get Wisdom and Knowledge from God

23. Hacking the Universe: The Revolutionary Way to Achieve Your Dreams and Unleash Your True Power

24. Holistic Psychology: 77 Secrets about the Mind That They Don't Want You to Know

25. How to Change the World: The Path of Global Ascension Through Consciousness

26. How to Get Lucky: How to Change Your Mind and Get Anything in Life

27. How to Improve Your Self-Esteem: 34 Essential Life Lessons Everyone Should Learn to Find Genuine Happiness

28. How to Study and Understand Anything: Discovering The Secrets of the Greatest Geniuses in History

29. How to Spot and Stop Manipulators: Protecting Yourself and Reclaiming Your Life

30. Intuition: 5 Keys to Awaken Your Third Eye and Expand Spiritual Perception

31. Karma Mastery: Transforming Life's Lessons into Conscious Creations

32. Legacy: How to Build a Life Worth Remembering

33. Master Your Emotions: The Art of Intentional Living

34. Mastering Alchemy: The Key to Success and Spiritual Growth

35. Metanoia Mechanics: The Secret Science of Profound Mental Shifts

36. Metamorphosis: 16 Catalysts for Unconventional Growth and Transformation

37. Mindshift: Aligning Your Thoughts for a Better Life

38. Mind Over Madness: Strategies for Thriving Amidst Chaos

39. Money Matters: A Holistic Approach to Building Financial Freedom and Well-Being

40. Quantum Leap: Unleashing Your Infinite Potential

41. Religious Leadership: The 8 Rules Behind Successful Congregations

42. Reset: How to Observe Life Through the Hidden

Dimensions of Reality and Change Your Destiny

43. Resilience: The Art of Confronting Reality Against the Odds

44. Raise Your Frequency: Aligning with Higher Consciousness

45. Revelation: The War Between Wisdom and Human Perception

46. Singularity: What to Do When You Lose Hope in Everything

47. Spiritual Anarchist: Breaking the Chains of Consensual Delusion

48. Spiritual DNA: Bridging Science and Spirituality to Live Your Best Life

49. Spiritual Warfare: What You Need to Know About Overcoming Adversity

50. Starseed: Secret Teachings about Heaven and the Future of Humanity

51. Stupid People: Identifying, Analyzing and Overcoming Their Toxic Influence

52. Technocracy: The New World Order of the Illuminati and The Battle Between Good and Evil

53. The 10 Laws of Transmutation: The Multidimensional

Power of Your Subconscious Mind

54. The 14 Karmic Laws of Love: How to Develop a Healthy and Conscious Relationship With Your Soulmate

55. The 33 Laws of Persistence: How to Overcome Obstacles and Upgrade Your Mindset for Success

56. The 36 Laws of Happiness: How to Solve Urgent Problems and Create a Better Future

57. The Alchemy of Truth: Embracing Change and Transcending Time

58. The Altruistic Edge: Succeeding by Putting Others First

59. The Antagonists: What Makes a Successful Person Different?

60. The Antichrist: The Grand Plan of Total Global Enslavement

61. The Art of Letting Go: Embracing Uncertainty and Living a Fulfilling Life

62. The Awakening: How to Turn Darkness Into Light and Ascend to Higher Dimensions of Existence

63. The Egyptian Mysteries: Essential Hermetic Teachings for a Complete Spiritual Reformation

64. The Dark Side of Progress: Navigating the Pitfalls of Technology and Society

65. The Evil Within: The Spiritual Battle in Your Mind Deception: When Everything You Know about God is Wrong

66. The Game of Life and How to Play It: How to Get Anything You Want in Life

67. The Hidden Language of God: How to Find a Balance Between Freedom and Responsibility

68. The Mosaic of Destiny: Deciphering the Patterns of Your Life

69. The Most Powerful Quotes: 400 Motivational Quotes and Sayings

70. The Secret Beliefs of The Illuminati: The Complete Truth About Manifesting Money Using The Law of Attraction That is Being Hidden From You

71. The Secret Empire: The Hidden Truth Behind the Power Elite and the Knights of the New World Order

72. The Secret Science of the Soul: How to Transcend Common Sense and Get What You Really Want From Life

73. The Spiritual Laws of Money: The 31 Best-kept Secrets to Life-long Abundance

74. The Spiritual Mechanics of Love: Secrets They Don't Want You to Know about Understanding and Processing

Emotions

75. The Universal Code: Understanding the Divine Blueprint

76. The Unknown: Exploring Infinite Possibilities in a Conformist World

77. The Narcissist's Secret: Why They Hate You (and What to Do About It)

78. Thrive: Spark Creativity, Overcome Obstacles and Unleash Your Potential

79. Transcend: Embracing Change and Overcoming Life's Challenges

80. Uncharted Paths: Pursuing True Fulfillment Beyond Society's Expectations

81. Uncompromised: The Surprising Power of Integrity in a Corrupt World

82. Unacknowledged: How Negative Emotions Affect Your Mental Health?

83. Unapologetic: Taking Control of Your Mind for a Happier and Healthier Life

84. Unbreakable: Turning Hardship into Opportunity

85. Uncommon: Transcending the Lies of the Mental Health Industry

86. Unlocked: How to Get Answers from Your Subconscious Mind and Control Your Life

87. Why do good people suffer? Uncovering the Hidden Dynamics of Human Nature

88. Your Full Potential: How to Overcome Fear and Solve Any Problem

89. Your Soul Purpose: Reincarnation and the Spectrum of Consciousness in Human Evolution

About the Publisher

This book was published by 22 Lions Publishing.

www.22Lions.com

Printed in the USA
CPSIA information can be obtained
at www.ICGtesting.com
LVHW051758301124
798014LV00001B/174